Creating Cultural Motifs against Terrorism

CREATING CULTURAL MOTIFS AGAINST TERRORISM

Empowering Acceptance of Our Uniqueness

Don J. Feeney Jr.

Westport, Connecticut
London

Library of Congress Cataloging-in-Publication Data

Feeney, Don J., 1948–
   Creating cultural motifs against terrorism : empowering acceptance of our uniqueness /
Donald J. Feeney, Jr.
     p. cm.
   Includes bibliographical references and index.
   ISBN 0–275–97920–2 (alk. paper)
   1. Social psychology. 2. Culture conflict. 3. Personality and culture. 4. East and West.
I. Title
HM1033.F43 2003
302—dc21   2003045600

British Library Cataloguing in Publication Data is available.

Library of Congress Catalog Card Number: 2003045600
ISBN: 0–275–97920–2

First published in 2003

Praeger Publishers, 88 Post Road West, Westport, CT 06881
An imprint of Greenwood Publishing Group, Inc.
www.praeger.com

Printed in the United States of America

The paper used in this book complies with the
Permanent Paper Standard issued by the National
Information Standards Organization (Z39.48–1984).

10 9 8 7 6 5 4 3 2 1

Connaître' c'est aimer
To know is to love
Dedicated to my daughter Kelly

CONTENTS

ACKNOWLEDGMENTS

I am deeply grateful to the many artists, educators, political scientists, and cultural psychologists who have influenced and guided me over years past. In addition, the learnings and cultural exposure acquired through such resources as the Chicago Council on Foreign Relations, the Art Institute of Chicago, Musée D'orsy, the Louvre, and the Institute of the Arab World in Paris have been invaluable.

In particular, I wish to highlight the significant contributions of Maria Mocuta, who is adjunct professor in the Department of Modern Languages at both De Paul University of Chicago and Loyola University Chicago. Her research on modern languages has appeared in such prestigious publications as the *Journal of Claudel Studies*. Dr. Mocuta's research at various colleges and universities, in particular her studies at the Sorbonne University in Paris, and her extensive international travels have intensified the value of her consultations regarding linguistic intricacies and cultural motifs.

Her research publication on Paul Claudel "L'oeil écoute" (The Eye Listens) is of particular significance as it focuses on visual-auditory synesthesia effects on artistic perception and interpretation. The experiential effect of synesthetic shifting among sensory systems reveals dual realities of literal and figural symbolism. These realities reflect emerging conjunctions arising in the interactive juxtaposition of creative cultural motifs.

Finally, I want to express my deepest gratitude to my daughter Kelly, exemplifying intrinsic commitment toward the exploration and cultivation of creative cultural motifs in her lifetime.

INTRODUCTION

The devastating events of 9/11 in America have raised the specter of terrorism as a permanent part of our lives. The incredulous horror that brought down the World Trade Center first appeared to be shockingly unreal, as if one were watching a B-rated science fiction movie out of Hollywood. Its all-to-real nature shattered our sense of what is normal and realistically possible. The new normal is that anything that is possible is probable. When the world's busiest airport in Atlanta was shut down because a man ran wildly through the airport, the vision of planes colliding with the World Trade Center's Twin Towers, and America's financial symbol of achievement crumbling in the aftermath, was hauntingly in everyone's thoughts. The overriding anxiety and terror has been "What's next!?" Heightened vigilance and shock affect judgment, perception, and reactivity levels.

There is an immediate need to come to terms with safeguarding our homeland from future horrors as well as to attach the source. There is also the need to grasp what conditions are essential and conducive to establishing a way of life in which our culture, as well as the world's, can be terror-free. It is to the latter that this work is focused.

Terrorism is symptomatic of a culture suffering from ill-formed identity boundaries and restrictive growth. Terrorism is the viral infection that rages within the weakened immune system of a culturally impaired organism. When the integrity and capacity of a culture's growth to harmoniously expand and diversify is severely limited and restricted, it will be vulnerable to the diseased invasions of fanatical, deviant forms.

The people (not the ruling regimes) of the Arabic culture continue to struggle to raise their standard of living. Their quality and level of education, economic growth, and cultural sophistication (e.g., arts, music, industrialization, and ability to compete in global markets with product diversification) is severely impaired. Powerful regimes (such as those in Saudi Arabia, Iran, and Iraq) have amassed enormous wealth, creating elite classism. Yet, their vast population remains underdeveloped, restricted, and impoverished in a substandard quality of life. It has been noted that the people of Israel have produced over 4,000 books as compared to barely 400 from the entire Arabic region (Zakaria, 2001). Despite oil-rich countries, the Arabic culture has yet to learn how to translate and transform their great wealth into quality improvements in their standard of living. Try as they may, no system of government has been found to effectively mobilize the Arabic countries toward a qualitative growth of its people. This may have a great deal to do with the oppressive nature of the ruling regimes. The cumulative result of all these conditions is a thriving breeding ground for terrorism.

This very breeding ground contributed to the tragic events of 9/11. Such a festering, cancerous growth as terroristic Islamic fundamentalism feeds on the cultural stagnation of the Eastern world. Cultural impoverishment in education, human rights, and artistic and industrial developments prevents a well-defined character structure and personality of their society to emerge. The underdeveloped cultural personality of the Eastern world has collided with an emerging global economy. The result is a highly charged, intimidating context for the underdeveloped Arabic peoples. Their intense fear and feelings of helplessness with the prospect of being overwhelmed by the technologically advanced Western cultures has positioned them in a cultural corner. Such cultural corneredness makes for dangerous, volatile conditions leading to distortions, misperceptions, and rigid fixations. It can give rise to a condition known as dysfunctional entrancement and can lead the way to rigid, delusional, irrational, and literal ways of thinking, believing, and behaving. (An example of this condition is crashing U.S. commercial airliners into the towers of the World Trade Center, believing there is a guaranteed reward of 72 vestal virgins in heaven awaiting such mass murder and self-annihilation.) It is important to realize that cultural stagnation leaves a society stunted and dwarfed in comparison to others. Powerful perceptual distortions and delusions can exist about the motivations of the West that can appear to justify (to a general population and especially to terrorists like Osama bin Laden) mass destruction and the murder of thousands of innocent civilians. These and other related issues including a forensic analysis of culturally stagnant personality development in the Eastern world will be explored in the following chapters.

Healing such a cancerous growth involves surgical removal of the cancer. It also involves healing and strengthening the constitutional integrity and boundaries of the cultural organism's immune system. This latter point is another theme of the chapters to follow.

There are two central themes of this work. The first is the concept that will be referred to as dysfunctional entrancement, mentioned earlier. It is the fanatical fixation of absorbed and trancelike attending and obsessions on narrow, irrational, and literal ways of thinking and behaving. Such a concept will be fully explored.

The second major theme is that of unique formative motifs. "Motif" is an artistic term referring to an artist's unique stylistic design and way of doing and expressing his or her art forms (e.g., Pablo Picasso's and Marc Chagall's motifs). It will be presented that all cultures have their own unique core themes and design structures that express idiosyncratic styles or motifs. The degree to which a cultural organism (America, Europe, Asia, Arabic countries) is healthy is the degree to which it can both align itself with its core motifs and evolve them in diverse, innovative ways without losing touch with its essential core roots.

The concept of Americanization is an example of a cultural motif that seeks to both stay anchored to its roots, yet expand and diversify in multiple, formative (variety of forms) ways. The Statue of Liberty text expresses this concept of formative motifs: "Bring me your weak, your blind, your foreign peoples ..." suggesting that American is "American" when it offers freedom of expression for all who want to come and bring to life their Americanized dream of being all that they can be!

It will be presented that when unique formative motifs of a culture are impaired, restricted, or truncated in their growth, then dysfunctional entrancement will emerge and weaken immunity and fanatical, terroristic infections will result.

The focus of this work is to consider Eastern and Western civilizations as vast networks of complex living forms (or formative ways of life) enjoined with evolutionary pressure to thrive and survive. Like all living formative entities, they need to grow and prosper in their own unique, idiosyncratic way or risk being stunted at the very least or annihilated at the very worst.

Accepting the proposition that the growth and prosperity of a particular living entity needs to be nurtured and cultivated, its deprivation will make it vulnerable to ill health, diseases, breakdowns and disintegration. Life is energy moving and flowing with a unique, formative intelligence. Restricting or cutting off such flowing, formative energies results in trees wilting, people getting sick, and cultures and civilizations shrinking and fading out of prominence and existence.

Terrorism is a disease or virus of a culture that is a restrictive force impairing the flow of formative growth. The need to nurture and cultivate a culture involves ensuring that its unique, idiosyncratic formative design (or motif) is enhanced and permitted to diversify like branches of a tree or trees in a forest or forests in a country (or countries in the world).

Because of globalization, countries and cultures are not only more interdependent but interactional. What this means is that boundaries of countries begin to blur as products, services, and even values tend to come from multiple parts of the world. The label "made in America" is somewhat misleading in that parts of a car are actually composed of pieces made in different countries even though sold in America (e.g., the Saturn from General Motors and Toyota).

The implications for the growth of formativeness in countries (and the cultures to which they belong) are that it requires resilience and confidence to sustain one's cultural identity when interactional effects are operating and lines and boundaries are blurred. As with the Saturn, it may be difficult to say what is made in America or Japan, or if these types of terms make any sense any more.

Sophisticated cultures learn to incorporate other cultures at what may be called a metalevel. This means going one level above conventional ways of making sense of things. One could say that America now means tolerating greater diversity and complexity going "meta" to other cultures. That is, one could suggest that including parts made by a Japanese country into an "American car" makes it even more American because it has gone meta (one step above) beyond a literal, set way of doing things. It has become more symbolic (or figurative) in what it means to be American. Its diversity makes it paradoxically more American.

The more things change, the more American they remain. While this is one of the great features of the United States of America and is its motif or idiosyncratic way of being, it also begs the question of what "Americanization" really is.

Cultures like the Arabic Islamic civilization don't have this quality of metalevel functioning where incorporating other's cultural styles and values can occur at symbolic levels. The way the Islamic culture treats its women, even those living in America, preserves certain limits and strictures of how to behave and dress. The capacity to go meta is not as operative in the Islamic culture (meaning Arabic-Persian culture) as it is in America.

As a result of these types of differences, tolerance in America for difference is actually more American, whereas for other cultures it can be intimidating and threatening. This is where cultural starvation begins to set in. When nurturance and development (e.g., general level of education, talent development, and standard of living) are impaired, Islamic cultures can feel dwarfed, overwhelmed, and stifled. The more undernourished and underdeveloped the culture, the more rigid, literal, and obsessive it will become (in order to survive the perceived threat). Such narrow, truncated fixations can create distortions about one's reality in the Islamic world (small, insignificant, helpless, etc.) as well as one's reality of the West (big, powerful, intimidating—and yes, even the land of the infidels).

Throughout the ages, there has been a battle of formativeness between Eastern (even the form of God—which one is He or Her or It or Thou or What?) and Western civilizations (e.g., the Crusades were the West's version of the holy wars). Yet, even in the thirteenth century, these excursions into cultural clashes were as much about material wealth, property, and quality of life in this world as about the metaphysical realities of the next world.

The chapters that follow will explore and elucidate how critical and essential it is to nourish and enhance cultural motifs in their own unique, idiosyncratic way. When creative comforts of food, shelter, and standard of living dwindle or other cultures expand with stunning achievements, perceived threats and imbalances can lead to fundamentalist fantasies of rigid, literal, and fixated distortions. It is at this point that the cancerous growth of terrorism can enter into the weakened immune system of a brittle, stagnant, atrophied culture. Violence and destruction result.

The evolution of cultural development throughout human history has involved physical violence and recurring cycles of war and peace. A key focus of this work depicts the inherent resourcefulness of enhancing unique formativeness in cultural motifs, revealing its collateral effect white moving toward the extinction of violence. Throughout the ages of human civilization, combativeness, warfare, and periods of peace have cycled endlessly. From Alexander the Great through Napoleon Bonaparte, there has been an ever-increasing reorganization of civilization and social-cultural design. The Roman Empire ruled the known world for hundreds of years and brought increasing benefits in social order. However, the price involved massive bloodletting, cruelty, and death. Violence has been the great means whereby the movement toward higher ordering in social-cultural systems has evolved. This work presents how emphasis on unique formativeness in motifs supplants the role of violence in generating higher social-cultural integration. It will be presented that emphasizing and nurturing formativeness in cultural motifs worldwide contributes toward diminishing violence. It is not about foreign aid that simply gives tools, food, and medical supplies. Rather, it is about identifying and nurturing what resources are necessary (guidance, mentoring, embracing cultural uniqueness through education and values clarification programs), to strengthen and articulate unique cultural motifs. It is to this end that this work is committed. Only in this way will all cultures have the global opportunity to discern their meaningful purpose in the world.

Chapter 1

DEVELOPING FORMATIVE MOTIFS IN TERRORISM-FREE CULTURES

The extraordinary nature of recent events has made it imperative to discern and delineate what sets of conditions and characteristics may best provide a terrorism-free culture. Recent studies at Yale University (Russett, 1993) and the Carnegie Committee for Science and Technology (Russett, 1992) have found that pluralistic and democratically oriented countries are least likely to engage in conflict and war.

It has been said that the tripod is the most stable of all geometric designs. The same may be said for countries and cultures that advocate diversity, democratic principles of life, and differentiation in self and cultural growth. Based on recent studies, it would appear that models and constructs emulating principles of pluralistic diversity and democratic ways of operating would be most successful in creating a terrorism-free culture.

The construct and functioning of what may be termed developmental motifs embodies core qualities of what research studies have suggested may be most successful in building terrorism-free cultures. It is to this end that the present chapter and those that follow are aligned.

Understanding motifs and their presence in cultures involves taking a panoramic perspective. The way a culture evolves is an expression of evolving life-forms of which cultures are but a formative version. Cultures are themselves an expression of formative evolution with their own unique, inherent motifs and designs.

Evolution is life expressing itself in an ever-expanding flow and diversity of multiple design structures known as motifs. Whether biological, psychological, sociological, cultural, or global, the hierarchy of organization can be of the infinitely small or infinitely large—from quantum mechanics to spiraling galaxies. All life-forms seek to perpetuate their own unique design structures or motifs in ever diverse ways. If they do not grow, then they risk nonexistence. Be it the simplest one-celled organism, the vast complexity of the human brain's neural net, or the nuanced, multifaceted nature of globalization, creatures and cultures seek to manifest and proliferate their inherent core nature. There may be fierce competition among living forms (e.g., animals, human beings, cultures) for survival. Rogoff (2003) has suggested that the nature of human growth (both biological and psychosocial) is intrinsically grounded in cultural development. Therefore, cultures can be construed as life-giving formativeness emerging from current behavioral patterns, rituals, and customs embedded in a defined group population or civilization. As cultures are evolving life-forms, (e.g., constant refinements and synergy in behavioral patterns and customs), they are dynamic and unique in their idiosyncratic variations in both the general population as a whole and the individuals within it. Examples of the former might be Americans residing in northern states as compared with those of southern states. Examples of the latter may be individuals raised in large families in a rural, nonindustrial area compared with those raised in small families in an urban, highly industrialized area. Yet, many times the existence of one life-form is interdependent with another. There are millions of what might be called good bacteria that help maintain health in the human digestive track. These good bacteria protect us from bad bacteria, such as *E. coli* and *Salmonella,* while our intestinal tract gives them a home in which to live.

As societies and cultures expand and become diverse, specialization becomes more prominent. Each part of a culture depends on the other for survival. America is so diverse and interdependent in its functioning that if one part thrives so will the rest. If the entertainment industry prospers, people will travel to be entertained, spend money to be part of it, and learn how to market it. By the same token, when an industry is functioning poorly, many others can also suffer (e.g., when people are afraid to fly, the domino effect on hotels, support-service workers, limousine operators, restaurants, catering companies, convention centers, Disney World, theme parks and so forth are all affected).

Societies and cultures function like complex mobiles where, when one piece is pulled, the rest begin to vibrate. These unique formative combinations of interdependent diversities interact and evolve into ever-complex motifs of a culture. Understanding the concept of cultural motifs first requires understanding what motifs are and how they emerge into a cultural domain. Only after comprehending motifs at the individual level will the implications of their synergistic, multifaceted formativeness become clear at the cultural level.

TRANSFORMING MOTIFS

Within each individual are inherent, self-organizing properties that constitute and consist of unique design structures (formative patterns). The composite integration of these design structures is the individual's motif (Feeney, 1996). The motif's inherent properties of self-organization are unique to each individual. The motif provides a novel perspective of a superstructure or epigenetic dimension incorporating but transcendent to both genetics and environment as a third force for transformation. Such a metastructure and framework articulate unique design structures within each individual, orchestrating genetic influences and selective, environmental interactions resonant to the uniqueness of each person. The orchestration of complex growth processes is propelled by unique, inherent properties of the human organism's capacity for design and structure at multiple levels of self-organization. The human brain, for example, self-constructs its own structures, accessing neural circuits and wiring and honing them to the task at hand (Eliot, 1999). Such properties involve capacities in the human organism for self-organization capable of generating idiosyncratic (uniquely individualized) design structures known as motifs.

THEMAS AND WEBS

Motif is the archetexture of self. Motif organizes and operates throughout the physical and psychosocial development of the individual. Motif is a constancy of unfolding change-states manifesting a family of coherent themas or design structures integrated into a weblike lattice of a complex whole. No one thema encompasses the whole, yet each thema interfaces and interconnects with the others, like individual threads of a web; when one is pulled the entire complex may resonate in whole or part of that entity. Themas are multifaceted, occurring throughout multiple levels of the organism. At one point in time, an individual may exhibit one formative thema (e.g., flexible, easygoing, and casual). At another point, he or she may exhibit other themas (compulsive, rigid attitudes; a demanding, formal nature). The degree of how themas overlap forms the interactive complexity of unique, emerging motif within that individual. The differential complexity of how an individual moves begins to emerge.

Notice the rich perspectives and modes of operating for someone who has encountered vast ranges of experience and wisdom over the years. His or her motif emerges much more readily than that of an individual with a limited variety of experiences. Varied experiences in living assist in the differentiation of themas and the emerging complexity of motif.

Themas or design structures represent multiple facets of each individual's unique personality, physiology, temperament, and psychosocial mode of functioning. Taken as a whole, these themas interact and integrate into a complex whole or weblike structure. Such weblike structures have unique design features characteristically represented and repeated with intersecting variations throughout multiple levels of the human organism. These weblike manifestations form unique motifs and indeed are the expression of the self's idiosyncratic motif. The complexity of human personality consists of motifs and their themas, which serve as organizing matrices and are influenced by the development of conceptual constructs of self and reality. These constructs are subjectively formed by the age of five and have been found to remain relatively consistent throughout the individual's life span, impervious to educational experiences though they are modifiable and evolve to maturational levels in the adult years (Restak, 1995). Such constructs as safety, how the world operates, who is trustworthy, ways of controlling oneself, what ideals to aspire to and so on are all created by the self at very early stages of development.

The tendency to develop, construct, and integrate one set of beliefs over another certainly is affected by the self's temperament and its interaction with the environment (James & Woodsmall, 1988). Yet, the presence of unique weblike structures of motif serves as a meta-organizing third force guiding the foundation for growth. Infused throughout the temperament of the individual and its self-selecting way of responding to environmental conditions and stimuli are inherent organizing principles operating behind the scenes at metalevels above both temperament and environmental interactions. The temperament of an individual represents predisposing orientations (e.g., extraversion, aggressiveness, sociability, tempo, and levels of emotional sensitivity). These can all affect cognitive interpretations of the self's interaction with the world. An individual with an outgoing, bold temperament may meet adversity as a challenge and strive to overcome it. Another individual, passive and sensitive with a tendency to feel things deeply, may struggle with adversity, feeling overwhelmed. Yet, operating behind the scenes for both types of temperament is the characteristic of uniqueness within these temperaments. Each individual has his or her own unique nuance, shade of meaning, variation, and tempo for how his or her temperament is constructed and manifest. It is to this unique specificity that one's idiosyncratic design structure or motif operates and is manifest.

It is the unique valence, weight, and intensity of how each thema participates that reflects the overall unique organizing principles at work. The degree, intensity, and juxtaposition of various themas and how they come together are similar to a recipe for a special dish or meal. Each of the ingredients has its own proportion, timing, and patterned combination, yet each meal is uniquely prepared by a master chef (representing inherent organizing principles of unique self motif) who follows no set recipe. Rather, an intuitive, artistic-level sense of what ingredients, in what proportion, combination, and sequence, would create that unique taste is the formativeness of the recipe. Each time the master chef prepares the exquisitely artful gourmet meal it is never exactly the same. With each new meal preparation, unique similarities emerge as the signature of the master chef but with subtle variations.

The uniqueness of patterning, the unique similarity of recipe in the complex whole design is the guiding motif within the temperament and among its selective, environmental interactions.

FORMATIVENESS IN PERCEPTION AND COGNITION

The motif's themas or design structures are not the self's constructs of reality or the belief system but rather the lattice or weblike skeletal framework upon which such cognitive operations are founded. The motif's themas influence the fundamental formation of the self's beliefs and constructs of reality. Beliefs and constructs of reality result in part from perceptual filters of incoming sensory stimuli and higher cerebral, cortical processing and interpretive analysis. This results in making deletions, distortions, and generalizations (James & Woodsmall, 1988) through sensory information processing. Involved is a formative reorganization of information into a meaningful design or motif. Through comparative analysis and cognizing stimuli (e.g., ordering, shaping, and organizing data), abstractions are delineated that organize information in relevant or meaningful ways to the individual. Thus, formation of beliefs and constructs of reality involves using a formative way of filtering, organizing, and integrating incoming data into a meaningful order. Developmentally, young children follow the Piaget stages of moving from sensory experience to concrete operational ideas and later to abstract formulations. This concrete to abstract development is essentially an organizational development of formativeness, which is exactly the function of motifs.

The unique way a young child deletes, distorts, and makes generalizations first involves perceptual filters that skew attention and interest of how incoming sensory data are ordered and grouped. For example, young children will give greater attention and show more positive emotion to symmetrical structures (Etcoff, 1999). In addition, novel stimuli of brightness, noise, movement, color and so on are more likely to capture a young child's interest than those lacking such features. How the child pays attention and experiences pleasant or unpleasant emotions to such stimuli contributes to what information is absorbed and how it may be positively or negatively labeled. As each child's brain is unique in subtle ways (Edelman, 1992), what is absorbing and attentive to one child may be boring and uninteresting to another. The way children organize their perceptual filters varies from child to child. Different dimensions of ordering (e.g., color; movement; sound; sequence; the gestalt or whole pattern of how stimuli may be arranged, either in terms of closeness or movement, groupings, or size) are all weighted slightly differently for each child.

The perceptual filters themselves are organized by the motif's themas, which therefore determine what is attended to and how the brain receives it. The individual child tends to perceive and conceptualize events in his or her reality according to his or her own motif design structures. The design structure of the midbrain's amygdala (known to be a center for emotions of fight or flight, arousal, and motor activity) affects its threshold level of sensitivity. Studies of four-month-old infants reveal that those who respond to novel stimuli (such as noise or the smell of alcohol) with high arousal of motor activity and irritability showed low thresholds of stimuli in their amygdalae. The effects of perceiving stimuli with such sensory perceptions and responses later translated into cognitions of danger, fear, and withdrawal as exhibited by right frontal lobe activity (dealing with negative emotional material) (Eliot, 1999). The design structure of sensory perceptions and activities translated into higher-ordering cognitions. The motif of perception translates into higher organizational levels of thought-form cognitions.

The mind-brain system of self designs itself through interactions both between its own neurons and with the external environment. Sensory touch affects and is affected by characteristic design structures in the mind-brain system. While there is adaptation to environmental sensory stimuli, such accommodation is achieved using characteristic motif designs of the assimilating mind-brain system. When confronted with extreme degrees of environmental variations (e.g., exaggerations in stimuli that significantly diverge from the preferred mode of perception and conception), the child has difficulty using his or her own rules of perception and cognition. Because the child's rules of organizing and structuring reality are primitive and underdeveloped, cases of extreme environmental events (emotional, physical, or sexual abuse) cause massive environmental discrepancy and conflict to their inherent modes of how to make sense of the world.

Dissonance of stimuli (e.g., a child who experiences conflict between his or her preferred design structure for soothing, low noise, soft lighting and loud, abrasive sounds) may contribute to negative emotional associations to certain perceptions. Environmental labeling by significant others (e.g., parents) can further skew what the child perceives as positive or negative. Parents who exhibit high levels of excitement, novelty, noise, and rapid change with their children may skew such experiences in positive or negative ways (laughing loudly or fighting violently), may arouse unique associations and interpretations depending on the child's preferred way of organizing perceptions (motif), and comparative analysis can create such formative ways of thinking as life is beautiful or life is dangerous.

The essential point is that the motif manifests its influence of structuring and ordering at both the perceptual and conceptual levels. When the young child takes in new experiences in his or her own way (filters data based on thema selectivity), ordering and perceiving them, this serves as information for the child's cerebral cortex to begin its deletion, distortion, and generalization process in creating beliefs and constructs of reality. The cognitive process of construction takes its cue from how the data were ordered, filtered, and perceived in the first place (Was it pleasant and harmonious or painful and clashing with the child's motif of preferred structuring?).

Through analysis and comparison, the executive functions (judgment, decision making, etc.) of the cerebral cortex analyze and compare what was experienced and how it was perceptually organized. That is, if the perceived experience had important features consistent with the inherent organizing motif of the child, a positive interpretation and construct would emerge. For example, the young child may perceive rapid movement, loud noise, harsh tones, and bright images in parents' or siblings' behavior and expressions. The child with a motif for slow tempo, easygoing movements, and subtle shades of sensory lighting may interpret his or her world as chaotic and painfully discrepant to personal needs. That child may develop beliefs of pessimism and helplessness. Such beliefs are interpretive, guided not simply by genetics or environmental interaction, but epigenetically by an organizing motif of the child's enjoying quiet, inwardly reflective sensations.

When confronted with discrepant and unpleasant perceived stimuli, the motif organizes that event from the slow-paced sensitizing, magnification perspective of inner reflectiveness. The motif inherently organizes and orients the young child to process the lack of resonance with an inner focus and reflectiveness, which, if not intervened, could induce or structure the child to develop depressive schemas. Notice, however, that the hidden influence of the motif's unique ordering is at work in affecting the probability of structuring which beliefs and constructs are likely to develop in light of the child's contextual experience. Even the context of the experience is actually framed by how the child structures his or her perceiving process of environmental experiences. Images formed from the way perceived filters (organized by the motif's themas) skew reality experiences can influence the formation of beliefs and constructs. The organizing effects of motif influence the perceptual process of darkness, silence, and ambiguous spaces in a child's bedroom at night, lending itself to cognitive distortions (creations). A child whose motif requires more structure, definition, and light would have such an experience.

Perceptions of this nature may exaggerate the quality of darkness and magnify shadows into figures that are cognitively structured into the personal meaning of a child whose motif's design requirements have not been met. In this case, the child might project the presence of monsters and gremlins and perceive that darkness is filled with unknown terrors.

Indeed, even adults prone to depression tend to use emotionally sensory-based reasoning. For example, upon awaking on a Monday morning, if one sees that the day is cloudy, one feels tired and disoriented and perceives it to be the beginning of a long, hard workweek. Such perceptions filtered and designed in this fashion induce an ordering of idea formation and symbolization suggesting a most negativistic emphasis. The person may construct the operating belief that he or she should just stay in bed. Notice that the person's motif emphasizes projecting throughout the whole week a sense of darkness and a personal feeling of disorientation (possible dizziness and lack of mental clarity).

If the person's organizing thema is one preferring to see the long-term nature of things, is linear in thinking, and seeks color and diversity, his thema requirements of color, diversity, and clarity are not met, which affects the construct and belief formation his motif now has formatted and influenced in the form of thema design structures.

Motifs influence through their design themas the rules of how perceptual and cognitive processes are to be framed and guided. Adler (Ansbacher & Ansbacher, 1956) addressed this issue, in part referring to the guiding rules of perception he called apperceptions. They are the structural lattice upon which percepts and cognitive thought-forms are self-constructed. Motifs function through their structuring process to increase the probability that their unique design formations and ordering filters will be adhered to. Such is the all-pervasive influence of motifs on mental function.

MOTIFS AND ARCHETYPES

The influence of motif is unique for each person. For example, the image formation that emerges from perceptions and cognitions influenced by motif is unique and archetypal for that individual self. Individualized images are the symbolic representations in their structure and design form (long tunnels, lightning speeds, tornadoes) of the unique self's themas and motifs. Such stimuli, for example, taken as a whole might suggest relativity of movement where one could be moving forward in one perspective or the lights and tunnels could be flashing by in another. This figure-ground reversibility can be an organizing motif thema that influences the schematic structuring the individual may use in multiple facets of his or her life tasks. (For example, figure-ground reversibility assists in peak performance, has motivational experiences, facilitates decision making, shares intimate experiences, and has dialogues.)

The self uses its unique core organizing design thema in an idiosyncratic manner that becomes a guiding archeidentity (or recipe) universal only to that individual. The motif's archetexture exists only in that individual self. Motifs have implications at higher mental levels of functioning. For example, motif's such as reversibility may have the further symbolic as well as structural impact, of affecting dimensions involving decision making, creativity, problem solving and the like. An individual with this unique type of motif may be able to perceive two sides of the same argument, shift back and forth in perspective, generate multiple creative perspectives, yet experience difficulty in deciding on only one outcome. The individual's motif (the particular way one uses reversibility, for example) is identical to no other and therefore goes beyond Carl Jung's (1971) universal archetypes.

The evolutionary nature of motif images (how the motif develops) is idiosyncratic to the individual and the images are, therefore, archeidentities to the unique signature of the person involved. Jung referred to universal archetypes from which all individuals draw. Yet, the uniqueness of the individual self is that idiosyncratic integration and formulation of all the individual themas or design structures evolving into the composite unique picture of motif. It is not unlike a Picasso painting with its myriad cubist fragments (or themas) juxtaposed into unique proportion and relationship to one another. This creates the unique priceless work of artistic motif of self.

The concept of archetype refers to the oldest archetextural design in history, that of the arch. It was used in ancient times to be the most efficient, all-pervasive, structurally stable design that could evenly distribute its weight load at 90-degree angles (right angles). The arch was considered the core stabilizing design element of the individual building structure. The literal and symbolic implications are obvious when we speak of core motifs as the archeidentity of the individual's all-pervasive sense of self in how it structures and carries the life load.

EVOLVING DESIGNS

The present being of each person's self is manifested and stabilized by the design, which also guides the becoming part of the self to unfold in precise but uniquely spontaneous ways. The motif designs movements that interact in unique fashion to create invariant variations (alternate variations of consistent uniqueness) of a transformative selfhood or being. This is similar to Martin Buber's "I-thou," where every thou is destined to become an it in an I-it relationship. This is a reified frozen quality of a thing divested of its unique flow and life-giving process. Every stage of the human existence is therefore destined toward moving from an I-thou to an I-it, or what may be termed positive disintegration, where the old breaks down in favor of new replacements. The process of being unfolded into that new being of becoming illustrates that change is constant in the motif's regeneration or renewal of selfhood.

The manifestations of self, self-identity, and self-concept are supported by the subtle substrates of the motif's archetextural process patterning that infuse these complex interactive flows of life themes in ways that may not always be apparent to the observing eye. Motifs are similar to the interweaving movements of a multisectioned orchestra where the conscious attention may be hearing one set of notes or another, yet it takes the entire range of consciousness to appreciate the full orchestrated flow of life movements in ways that create that artistic musical score of unique human selfhood. Motifs many times present the residual effects of the interacting life patterns or movements, like the figure emerging from the ground of their interactiveness. Such figure-ground emergence is guided by the self-motif's archetextural design inherent in the nature of selfhood. Manifestation of motifs can be seen and experienced when viewed from the ground of that creative system interacting in an open and creative process with itself and with the environment at hand. Many times the symmetry of the motif's patterns may emerge in asymmetrical imbalanced ways, illustrating its growth and evolutionary nature.

Motifs have a heterogeneous nature: They are not pure but rather involve a vast variance or even deviance in an ever-unfolding, at times imperfect mixture of the human being, the environment, and the becoming process. The motif is not rigidly fixed like something set in stone. Rather, it is an evolving, self-creating, interactive dynamic that moves in a holistic self-constructing, self-assembling way. Motif grows and refines itself from the interactions of the individual, the environment, and the multiple processes in which it occurs. Motif is never a pure form any more than there is an ideal signature to an individual or an ultimate form. Rather, the motif is hinted at, approximated, and always in the process of becoming yet another "ideal." The motif presents the ideal only for the moment of expression in that time, in that place, in that context just as a signature of human being reflects mood, state of mind, and the type of environmental influences one is currently experiencing. Such illusory and suggestive manifestations of the facets of motif are indicative of its hidden archetextural infrastructure, which is something that is never complete, but always evolving. It is an archetexture of hidden order embedded in the chaotic life of evolving events of growth, change, and evolution. It is nonplatonic but rather what the Greeks term *entelechy*, where the essence of the acorn is realized in the becoming of the oak tree.

Motif is not part of the self, it is the whole, unique essence of self. Motif is the archetextural infrastructure, unique and evolving through multiple levels: metabolic, sensory, biochemical, psychosocial, and so on. The motif is similar to the holograph in that no matter how many times it is broken down into pieces, each piece reflects the whole. In other words, no matter what one does or experiences, one cannot not be oneself.

Expansion in articulation of the grace and beauty of one's own unique, passionate endeavors allows one to discover the motif manifesting itself in remarkable clarity and consistency, offering peace, joy, and harmony in the years to come. As people evolve, they articulate and integrate their motif in everyday life in an aligned and attuned fashion. Anything short of the uniqueness of the articulate self is simply a fragmentation or larger part of what has been previously called temperament or character traits.

The motif manifests the cutting-edge, self-organizing uniqueness of self emerging from the field forces of environment and individual. It orchestrates the self-convergence and transformation through a quantum leap from the science of who human beings are to an artistic appreciation of what they have always been.

Motifs offer a healing quality. The more human beings align with motif, the greater behavioral and psychosocial benefits emerge in their environment. This result promotes wholeness, balance, and harmony in healing. Alignment with motifs reduces stress and converts pressures and influences into what may be called eustress. It provides an entrainment of the organism where one's inner core design begins to match and mirror the synergistic connection with appropriate people, places, events, opportunities, and capacities that enhance the manifestation of motif in everyday life.

Motif is not a core thing or place. It is an evolving archetexture guided by the boundary and outlines of the self/other contrast and articulates comparison and distinction between the two. It is neither subjective nor objective but the unique archetextural field or medium through which the self is an inherent oneness. It is common to think of being in or out of something observing or being observed. Yet, motif is neither the observed nor the observer, but could be both. The transformation is the self moving as one. Motif is at the cutting edge of the uncommon boundary of unfolding self-design. As such, it is always at one with itself yet capable of almost infinite unique variations.

When an individual's unique motif of design structure is accessed and resonated, deep levels of rapport and relatedness can be established. Interfacing with motifs in communication involves attunement to the complex organizing design structure of how an individual nonverbally communicates. This attunement involves refining attention and focus to just the right balance of sensory design organization, capturing the quality of artistry and the relational attributes of how individuals sensorially articulate and symbolize their movements, tonal sounds, points of emphasis and so on. Far from simply pacing another's rhythm, resonating with motifs involves grasping their unique hieroglyphic structure, symbol, and form. This may involve an infinite number of patterned and varied sequences of short, medium, or long movements, frequencies, intensities, durations, juxtapositions of phonemes and so on. Such grasping of motifs in communication is nothing short of resonating with the artistry and form of a master (e.g., Pablo Picasso and Marc Chagall). In each individual's case, such resonance manifests artistic mastery of oneself.

DEVELOPMENTAL MOTIFS

Persistence of an organizing motif (the self's signature) emerges developmentally throughout an individual's lifestyle. Pearce (1986) uses Piaget and Inhelder's work (1964) on early childhood development (concrete to abstract formal operations), suggesting emergence of a postbiological ego identity (Erikson, 1950). Pearce states that this identity emerges through development of sensory-motor connections and emotions toward a fluid mental world of creative power and expression. He notes that this organizing identity exists from the beginning of life but in a latent form that awaits, as a growth blueprint, stage-specific attention and development. He stresses the critical importance of models (motifs) essential for development of this identity blueprint or organizing principle.

The preceding material implies that individuals are inherently designed with a motif and intent to harmoniously organize their lives to be healthy and whole. Dabrowski (1967, 1970) and Dabrowski and Piechowski (1977) describe personality development as a progression of five ascending levels. They describe dynamic dimensions facilitating this ascendant self-organization as guided by a personality ideal, creating harmonious unity and integration. The inherent guiding unity of this personality ideal is characteristic of innate motifs and their intent toward unifying wholeness. The unique character of sensory motifs represents the personality that is ideal for that individual self.

Sensory motif is an inherent kind of structural schematic that determines the shape or design of what makes each of us unique. It is ever unfolding. The motif seems to operate as a highly individualized field of energy characterized not by a single pattern or even sets of patterns (in terms of personality and behavior patterns), but rather generates what is referred to as a family of interacting patterns. Human beings can be quite complex, and no single pattern or sets of patterns adequately describe the uniqueness of self. That is why most individuals resist being categorized. I advocate using the model of a family of interactive patterns as a step to grasp this complexity.

Such a model suggests that human beings operate in inherent patterned ways, modifiable at the behavioral level, yet essentially unchangeable at the core level of self. It is rather like the structure of a tree. The core pattern of the trunk is innate, yet the way it grows and branches outward is modifiable. The unique subtleties in inherent patterns of behavior (speaking, walking, working, loving, relating, etc.) in various areas of an individual's life overlap in their similarity yet express their own specific variations. Such a system of interactive patterns is referred to as a family of interactions. Our work behavior patterns affect and interact with our patterns of relating at home. Yet, the way we operate at work is not identical but only similar to our behavior patterns at home. (We may be high achievers at both home and work, but be more active at work and passive at home.) Our early childhood behavior and belief patterns interact with and affect the way we function as adults. Unique ways in which patterns in one area of our life affect those in other areas (thought and behavior patterns of love and intimacy learned in childhood affect and are affected by those adult learning experiences) demonstrate the interactive effects of sensory motifs.

The wholeness of the motifs lies buried in the myriad patterns and events of a person's life. It is not unlike asking how many faces you can see hidden in a picture collage of objects and figures. Sometimes standing back, releasing old fixations and opening up to creative ways that reformulate how and what a person is perceiving allows these motifs to emerge. That is why perceiving the family of interactive patterns is so essential in grasping how the motif is perceived. This allows the configuration of the motif to be visible.

These configurations are like the ripple effects of dropping a pebble into a pond. As patterns of waves spread out, some hit the shore and bounce back into oncoming patterns of waves. The interaction and interference effects of these colliding waves create shapes and configurations that repeat themselves in similar but different ways. Such similar but different configurations are called a family of interactive patterns. As motifs are not learned but are inherent structures to be developed, these interactive patterns are the distilled, pure manifestations of what is already innately present.

A very simple example of this can be seen in your own signature. Each time you sign your name, there will usually be some kind of small or large variation in the way you signed. However, you can always recognize your signature from anyone else's, as there are characteristics and shapes that emerge from the patterned variations of all of your signatures combined.

The sensory motif manifests itself in such a family of interactive patterns. Motifs imply unique configurations based on movement. We are always in movement whether we remain in one place or are quite active. Without movement, there is no life. However, the type of movement to which I refer is a special one known as flow. Csikszentmihalyi (1990) discusses how flow occurs through focused sensory and mental interaction, creating qualities of various form and design (e.g., a tennis player's flowing, back-and-forth movement exhibiting form, skill and art). All people may find their self-existence in flow experiences that evoke qualities of form and art where they say they really feel alive and exist as their true selves. The sensory motif's existence in self is essential for each person's unique sense of meaningful existence. It is equivalent to the essence of self.

Motifs most clearly demonstrate their unique configurations and characteristics in these flow states. Interactive motifs usually, but not always, involve exchange in various activities—either alone, as in reading a book, or with someone else, as in playing Ping-Pong or making love. Flow is a process that is conducive to generating a family of interactive patterns. That is why such a process is so intrinsically rewarding and gratifying. As a result, there is a powerful sense of purpose generated in these states.

Resonance between an individual's unique sense of self and the way one's lifestyle is manifested has been measured as meaning in life. Ebersole and Quiring (1991) discuss meaning in life depth (MILD) as a cognitive content process by using a five-point scale to measure depth of meaning. They indicate that the more precisely interactions of self and environment resonate to that person (i.e., the design qualities or motifs), the greater the sense of meaning. It is postulated that the self has unique form and design qualities that necessitate resonant interactions (such as art and music) idiosyncratic to that self's motif. Experience takes on meaning in terms of what one discovers as identifiable external forms that are symmetrical with internal organizing principles. As the individual experiences a matching of external and internal organizing experiences, he or she feels a sense of meaning and purpose in life.

Frankl (1963) has emphasized the importance of discovering meaning and purpose in life in logotherapy. Each person's organizing properties seem to have a unique differential signature (or designation) such that some experiences will resonate more with some individuals than with others. When there is resonance, the individual feels like there is purpose in his or her self-experience. This, therefore, can be referred to as a purposeful self that resonates or relates when symmetry is discovered in experiences that present properties of their organizing principle. This ordering process, although unique to each client, is essential for the joy of flow experiences to occur in such unself-conscious manifestations (Csikszentmihalyi, 1990). At such times, the individual has a sense of joy, absorption, or fascination.

Motifs can be expressed in flowing, artistic forms that are sequenced in unique, sensory syntax. The particular shape or configuration of a person's motif will have unique expressions. For example, some people may use such phrases as "see how they feel about ideas" or "get feelings off their chest." They then begin to share them verbally or auditorily. This could be their syntax of experience.

However, motifs are more than how the senses are sequenced. Motifs are an intricate and articulated type of design that partners begin to manifest in their own life characters. Motifs go beyond mere interests and hobbies. They are the structurally unique signatures of self. Motifs are the templates that generate within us an innate sense of order and beauty. They serve as the organizing gyroscopes that order the syntax of experience. They are fluid, not fixed. They involve a subtle, flowing order and creative design. As a result, they create a sense of purpose. This sense of purpose emerges as these flow states are experienced and transformed into their own unique artistry, form, and style of expression. Motifs can be seen in people flowing through some interaction. Yet, motifs are more than a style of interacting. There is a unique signature and blueprint in their characteristic ways of moving through life.

For example, some people may become very absorbed and intrigued in abstract symbols of ideas. Albert Einstein was one of those. In developing his theory of relativity, he would become absorbed and intrigued in what he called thought experiments. That is, he would imagine what the effect of time and space would be if he were riding a beam of light to the ends of the universe and back. His motif was one of manipulating abstract symbols in relative frames of reference where time and space are fluid. Such a motif involved contrast and juxtaposition of different levels of abstraction. Notice the interplay of an absolute, universal oneness contrasted against his emphasis on how relative the universe can be. Indeed, he sought oneness throughout his life as evidenced by his search for a unified field theory of universal forces. His penchant for relative frames contrasted beautifully with his search for pure truth and a universal constant ($E = mc^2$). His motif used a paradoxical structure as he pursued unification through relativity. It is interesting that his motif of enjoying the relative nature of a holistic universe never got him to dinner on time with his wife. He was late, but then it's all relative. Einstein enjoyed the motif of juxtaposing parts and wholes in contrasting designs. These designing features have a kind of architecture (or archetexture of feeling) in that they act as self-organizing templates. They serve to catalyze and guide the formulation and precise articulation of how these unique patterns can be expressed and experienced in the here-and-now situation. Each person has an intrinsic motif or family of interactive sets of qualities. To the degree to which we are congruent and aligned with sensory motif as an organizing principle of self, the more empowered, harmonious, and robust will be our relationship with ourselves and with others.

The organizing, empowering experience of motif allows fears, terrors, and anxieties to peak and then become incorporated into a larger, holistic, self-organizing identity. One's sensory motif is the experience of an immutable, unshakable reality of self at the core level. It therefore empowers and energizes awesome capabilities of belief, positive expectation, and creative imagination for problem solving. It gives one a sense of permanence in an otherwise chaotic world of trauma and turmoil. The degree to which the self can access and resonate with its own character or motif through outside interaction (Csikszentmihalyi, 1990) is the degree to which meaning and purpose are fulfilled.

The motif is an open system responsive to fluctuations in nuances, sensations and feelings, perceptions, memories and cognitions. It seems to emerge as an interaction between the inherent organizing character of the individual and the environment in which learning occurs.

The intricate organizing principles of sensory motifs can be seen when people are doing their life work. Whatever their field of experience (music, art, business, machinery, etc.), their choice expresses their unique internal organizing principles and manifests their movement in a flow state of purpose.

The experience of this organizing movement within the client when accessing such uniquely personal experiences is a feeling of "I cannot *not* do this." It is this principle of self-organization as manifest in sensory motifs that aligns the person's resources. This is similar to what Pearce

(1986) indicated when discussing the need for models to develop identity. It is alignment and resonance within this larger organizing field that facilitates the individual's empowered mental and sensory integration.

MOTIFS: SOUL AND SPIRITUALITY

The uniqueness of an individual is manifest through his or her idiosyncratic artistic motif. Such unique artistry of motif is imbued throughout the multiple levels of body-brain-mind and psychosocial dimensions. Moving from one dimension to another (body to brain, brain to mind, mind to family, mind to meaning) represents a transduction (transfer of formative information) from one medium to another.

Motif provides a formative "bridge," translating meaningful information design structures from one medium level to another. They are holographic, retraining the uniqueness of the motif's design structures resonating throughout internal and external levels of individual and psychosocial contexts. Movement from one level of organization to another is facilitated by the unique artistry of the self's motif. This includes movement to the next level or dimension known as soul and spirituality. Interfacing throughout this all-pervasive medium of mediums presumes one has evolved in personal growth and maturation through previous levels. Such evolution involves progressive alignment and resonant articulation with one's ever-expanding, unique motif. Accumulation of alignment and resonant growth is similar to the concentric rings within a tree trunk. For every year of tree growth, there is a larger ring that expansively encircles all the inner circles that represent previous years of growth. The unique design structure of the most expansive outer ring (which is not a perfect circle) builds upon previous circular designed rings, each with its own unique variations and derivations. Yet, there is a similar pattern or motif moving through each of the rings, connecting them in some resonant fashion. Such holographic, patterned movements are representative of the tree's inherent, organizing motif. Upon such accumulation and maturation, the individual can now seek to expand to the next expansive rung on the developmental ladder, that of soul and spirituality. There are distinctive, unique motifs in energy and spirit that formatively flow through the soul of self. The articulation of distinguishing formativeness strikes at the heart and soul of core self.

Depiction of soul in human beings extends formative motifs into highly refined states of articulation. As the human being evolves, internal, formative patterns progress from large, gross levels of expression (two- and four-celled divisions of the zygote known as blastula and gastrula) to refined, internal articulations (millions of intricate neural pathways in the brain's cortex).

Such pathways articulate intricate artistic design structures enabling complex altered states of mental functioning to arise. Crick alludes (in Searle, 1997) to these complexities in describing emergent properties of the brain evolving into mind function. Evolution of complex mind-body articulations allows the self's unique, formative motif exquisite expression. Manifestation of the motif's complexity to such a degree strikes at the very soul of self. Soul is not so much a complex function of mind as it is one of mindfulness, which articulates formative, holistic states of being. The greater the manifestations of unique motifs, the deeper the access to the soul. Yet, soul (and spirit) are present at all levels of self and can be awakened through resonating with unique motifs imbued throughout these levels.

The soul's ability to symbolize and inject the uniqueness of individual motif into seemingly inane events is the living miracle of the soul's animation of meaningfulness on life. Through attending to the soul, one can learn to discern meaning and purpose in an otherwise empty and inanimate, thing-oriented, materialistic way of life. Soul attending involves seeing the material world with soft eyes opening to multidimensional enrichment. One Reiki healer depicts seeing with the eyes of the soul in the following passage: "When you can see other dimensions—observe them through physical eyes with the aide of your third or perceptive eye [the third eye is the energy center or chakra located in the center of the forehead]—you know that which is heavy in light force and that which is light—you see slow moving low vibrations and fast moving high vibrations—to look at the flowering bloom of spring trees and it makes your heart flutter and you can literally feel it dance in your chest" (Feeney, 2000).

Motif is the essence of such unique formativeness. Motif is the artistic movement that details the magnificent recognition of nuanced color schemes in a sunset, the miracle of child raising, and the exquisite agony of loss and the self-resurrection that happens once you move on, emerge, and grow from that loss. It is the individual's unique way of creating formative order and meaning out of chaos. If life is a set of Rorschach cards (inkblots), then motif is the creative mode of construction. Each person selects and constructs in his or her outer world the embodiment of his or her inner motif. One sees the motif of the soul in the uniqueness of one's artistic creations.

The soul's sacredness can be expressed as a working or crafting of one's artistry. Moore (1992) refers to Plato's expression *techne tou biou,* "the craft of life," in depleting the sacred craft or artwork of the soul. If art is the soul's sacredness, then motif is the soul of its artistry. The soul's motif is the artistry of one's uniqueness crafting itself in the large and small events of one's life. The skill and attention involved in such crafting require sensitivity to one's sensory experience of self as well as observation of the world at large.

Attentiveness to nuances and subtleties in observing such events as a child playing, sunsets, swimming, lovemaking, and cleaning house activates unique sensory experiences of the moment-to-moment unfolding. Meaning and flow unfold in keen attention and sensitization in the art and craft of being one's unique self in the mindfulness of the moment.

The soul's motif crafts moment-to-moment encounters as brilliant unfolding improvisations of unique, formative manifestations. As such, walking through the woods becomes an I-thou encounter of renewal (Buber, 1958). The light through the trees, the wind, the smell of fresh pinecones—all unveil a beautiful cacophony unfolding as if for the first time. Intensity and vividness infuse the experiential encounter as the senses come alive in unique, formative observations. Learning to see and experience daily and life events as if for the first time (the child's innocence of fresh observance) unveils the uniqueness of ourselves as manifest in the uniqueness of what is before us. For some, the beauty and mosaic designs of a peacock's tail or a colorful rainbow may convey the soul of their motif. For others, it may be the brilliant flash of lightning or whitewater rapids of the Colorado River. Each person manifests his or her soul's motif in deeply personal, unique ways of observing, engaging, and infusing symbolic and creative improvisations. The ubiquitous, formative expressions available to each individual parallel his or her soul's motif of artistic expression. The possibilities are omnipresent at the soul's level of unique, artistic motifs.

Motif is an artistic concept in itself referring to a style and set of themes in how one's creative art is manifest. The soul's artistry has its motif reaching the depths of universal and spiritual sacredness. At such far-reaching depths and breadths of formativeness, accessing one's soul motif resonates with the omnipresence of spirituality. It is with such resonance that the soul's motif embraces and embodies the sacredness of spirituality.

UNIQUE MOTIFS AND RELIGION

Uniqueness of motif can be found in the various religions of the world. Major religions of the world are grounded on similar, all-encompassing truths (monotheism, ascendance toward higher levels of being, union and oneness, etc.). Yet, each of the major religions (Christianity, Judaism, Islam, and Hinduism) manifests its own unique meaning and facet of spirituality.

Kenneth Woodward (2000) quotes the philosopher George Santayana, who expresses the marked idiosyncrasy of each healthy, living religion. The unique message embodied in each religion conveys a special and surprising message through "the bias which that revelation gives to life." New vistas and mysteries revealing other worlds are available through each of the world religions. Therein lies the unique motif of each particular religion capturing mysterious and wondrous visions of dimensions and realms of realities far beyond common sense experience.

Through the description of miracles occurring in various religions' historical accounts, Woodward (2000) describes the unique meaning and message that miracles reveal in each religion. He describes miracles as stories and accounts of events that only make sense within larger-than-self realities.

Christianity's God of the New Testament is different from any other. The New Testament reveals the Holy Trinity of God as the Father, Son, and Holy Ghost (Spirit). Jesus Christ emerges as grounded within all three facets of the Trinity of God. Other distinctions can be discerned between the Tanakh (Hebrew Bible) and the Christian Old Testament. In the former, the Scriptures are sequenced and designed with a perspective of the coming of Christ fulfilling the Hebrew prophecy.

The progressive disappearance of miracles in the movement from Old to New Testaments is cast in a different light. Jesus used more miracles than prior prophets. The Matthew writings depict the view of Jesus Christ as the new Moses. This can be understood through His teachings, signs, and wonders (miracles). Jesus surpasses Moses from the gospel perspective, presenting Himself as possessing miraculous power reserved only for God. Moses hears the voice of God. As scriptures developed, there was a shift from God speaking directly to prophets toward Him speaking indirectly through them. His prophets and eventually His Son spoke for Him. This is an interesting development in religion. It is as if God's voice became more differentiated and uniquely expressed as time evolved. This is not unlike the evolution and differentiation of unique motifs. The unique complexity of each religion's faceted perspective of spiritual infinity offers rich diversity and differentiation in the unfathomable realms of omnipresence.

The critical elements of motif that contribute to a culture free of terrorism involve the quality of formativeness. It is this essential feature that will be the focus of the next section as motifs are now considered at the level of a cultural personality.

MOTIFS AND THE CULTURAL PERSONALITY

Cultures have motifs inherent to themselves because they are composed of collections of individuals who themselves have inherent motifs. The interplay between individual and cultural motifs involves a synergistic effect. When a collective of unique individuals comes together in some formative, mutually interactive way, there is fashioned something more holistic and multifaceted than its individual members. This can be seen in our forefathers who wrote and signed the Constitution of the United States. The Constitution is the inherent, multifaceted motif each of our forefathers fashioned and forged together as their synergistic whole. Neither Benjamin Franklin, John Hancock, nor Thomas Jefferson, by themselves, had the necessary and sufficient ideas, constructs and formative qualities encompassed in the totality of the United States Constitution.

The United States Constitution therefore is a holistic, multifaceted formative motif. The Constitution constitutes cultural motifs of the United States of America. It has evolved from unique interfacing (interfacation) of selective aspects of each of our forefather's individual motifs. The United States Constitution is our formative archetextural design structure of America's cultural motif and core personality. It has tremendous formativeness, as exemplified by the formative interpretations of the United States Supreme Court. In some ways, it is not unlike a Rubik's Cube. Certain sides of each colored square need to simultaneously align with certain sides of the other colored squares. Formative motifs operate to serve multitasked challenges especially at the cultural level. The United States Constitution needed to be articulated in the broadest way to encompass all the people in the least restrictive way.

Constitutions of cultures need to incorporate select facets of their own forefathers so as to be multifaceted and serve as a foundation of evolutionary formativeness for future generations.

The United States Constitution is forged with a multifaceted set of formative constructs and principles designing how individual human beings can live together with inalienable rights. Yet, its applications and implications need a Supreme Court to interpret how unique situations embody and manifest these principles of people's rights and values. Witness the recent presidential election, the Florida vote recount issue, and how it ultimately required the United States Supreme Court to resolve the "constitutionality" of the Florida recount. This is a classic example of how such a multifaceted motif needs to be derived in its most nuanced formative design structure. The real life experience of formative motifs being derived and applied in the most refined of artistic ways is the resulting election of George W. Bush as president. Whatever your politics, the United States Constitution served as a generative motif from which was fashioned a unique, artistic, refined resolution. Indeed, one could say that our president is a real piece of artwork. Motifs generate derivative artistic resolutions. In cultural motifs, there need to be freedom and openness for artistic, innovative derivations to manifest themselves.

Western civilization as we know it requires the innovative, evolving complexity of technological advancement to manifest greater mastery of itself and its universe. The unique formative evolution of such advancement can be seen in the ever-innovative information-computerization process occurring in both America and Europe. One could even characterize a kind of cultural personality evolving in such a mind-set. The rugged individualist of America has become even more interdependent on advancing technology and information flow to exert a sense of control and mastery on one's environment. The characteristics of bigger, better, and more and more choices are uniquely American and served by these advancements.

There can also be a kind of cultural personality with a European nuance. While functioning more as a group collective, the struggle to enhance production without losing the quality of group collectivity is a major theme in European countries. The need to excel and enhance the cultural personality of a country or civilization requires building on its unique, formative identity in innovative ways consistent with its inherent core nature. This is the challenge. A culture needs to build on its unique life formativeness in ways that offer innovative variations on core themes of that culture's personality. America is racing ahead with technological innovations, building ways in which more people can master more freedom and control in their individual lives.

The European community has also initiated innovations building upon unique, formative motifs of its cultural personality. One of the characteristics of the European cultural personality is the ability to operate in communal groups. They tend to feel more comfortable working as a team as opposed to individuals. Innovations of such motifs can be seen in such advancements as moving from multiple currencies toward a collective universal currency of the euro.

This chapter has introduced the construct of motifs and the need for formativeness in cultures to be free of terrorism. The next chapter focuses upon challenges and threats to formative cultural motifs and the dire consequences of cultural stagnation. The implications of underdeveloped countries with truncated cultural motifs vulnerable to outside consumption will be explored as a breeding ground for global terrorism.

Chapter 2

CHALLENGES TO MOTIFS' FORMATIVENESS: THE SEEDS OF TERRORISM

It is important to realize that cultural motifs are particular in their refinement, precision, and subtle nuance. For example, there is a class of languages known as Romance, which are essentially derived from Latin. These include English, French, Spanish, and Italian. They all use a common 26-character alphabet and have many similar word roots. In English, the word "question" uses a "ques" letter grouping. This same grouping can be found in French, for example, "qu'est," and in Spanish, "que es." In each case, both the phonetic sound and written word are similar and are used to make inquiries—to ask "ques"-tions. Yet, in each language, there are subtle refinements that elucidate unique signatures or motifs, idiosyncratic to that particular language. The English (American) version of asking or inquiring uses the obvious word "question." In French, the similar, but unique, derivative is "que'est" meaning "What is...?" and in Spanish the derivative is "que es." The French use the "kess" sound and the Spanish use the "k-es" sound. There is a merger of sounds in French, which doesn't appear Spanish and English (e.g., "question" is "q-wess-shion." These differences are admittedly slight, yet to the uninitiated, can play havoc in communication.

When I was in Paris, I inquired as to the location of the Arc de Triomphe. The French word "triomphe" is pronounced "tree-uanh." As I had pronounced it as "tri-umf," I received looks from the French as if I was from another planet (being from America may be their equivalent). It is just these subtle differences that can make and create major difficulties in communicating and comprehending one another. Such unincorporated differences can lead to irritation, hostilities, and, in Europe, a history of war. If such small differences can contribute to conflicts and warring carnage, imagine the vast cavern of difference between Eastern and Western language systems. Is it any wonder we consider each other the infidel?

The construct of unique motifs is used in describing artistic styles (e.g., Picasso's or Beethoven's style). As in the world of art, cultural motifs are powerfully affected by the slightest variations. In Beethoven's Fifth Symphony, the "da da dom" motif just wouldn't be the same if it was played "da da dee." Minor distinctions in musical notes, phonetic word sounds and so forth make or break the integrity of the unique formative motif. One subtle shift in word phonic (or accent) or musical notation can make the difference between a masterpiece and junk.

Many times certain ideas and subtle themes expressed in one language are difficult, if not impossible, to translate into another language. For example, the Eskimos have over one hundred words to describe variations in cold temperatures. It is very difficult to translate many of these into English. There are just no English words to describe some of these more subtle distinctions.

If people from America who have not studied languages in France, Spain, or Portugal have no idea of what is being said, and all these languages are derived from a common Latin root, how much more difficult must it be to understand languages and cultures of radically different root stems (motifs that are themselves derivatives of even larger motifs)? These larger motifs may be the untapped roots of global motifs.

The Arabic, Chinese, Japanese, and Russian alphabet characters are distinctly different from the Romantic language characters. In addition, while in the latter reading and writing go from left to right and top to bottom, other languages may move from right to left or in columns from top to bottom.

The point to all of this is that language and the countries and cultures from whence they come can seem so different that they may seem foreign (which in fact they are) to the unique cultural motifs in which one is raised. If common roots and similarities of expression are not found, different cultures can seem intimidating and threatening to one's unique way or motif of cultural life. It is at this point that cultural life-forms can come into cultural collision and the apparent struggle for survival emerges.

Cultures need to flourish, expand, and diversify. This process is known as formativeness and requires safe, nourishing environmental enrichment for stimulation and innovation. Intriguingly enough, one of the best sources for this enrichment is exchange with other diverse cultures. Foreign exchange programs enrich the formativeness and cultural innovations of one another's motif.

There is a caveat to such enrichment. Cultures lacking a healthy constitutional character identity and developmental framework can be swallowed up and consumed by those that are highly sophisticated and advanced. Such a threatening condition can occur in obvious cases of overt warfare. Napoleon's France and Hitler's Germany are blatant examples of one way of life attempting to consume another's. The English empire of the eighteenth and nineteenth centuries seeking to expand its domain into Africa and India further exemplifies the infusion of unique formative motifs of one culture into many others.

Cultural motifs have a personality that craves and hungers for enrichment from diverse sources. This can be done in healthy ways as long as some balance and set point can be sustained preserving the integrity of cultural roots and innovative wings. The set point is the degree to which a cultural motif can interface with others without losing its integrity. Equally important is the idea that underdeveloped countries and cultures need time and space to safely develop without being overwhelmed by advanced ones.

The threatening nature of one culture consuming and absorbing another into its domain is always the risk when establishing interactive exchanges. As long as cultures can remain separate and distinct, each is protected (though still enriched) from potential consumption. It requires well-refined and differentiated cultural motifs to sustain multicultural diversity without losing formative uniqueness. Lacking such well-formedness, cultures may radicalize (through fundamentalist movements) to achieve distance and distinction.

When cultures are threatened, they tend to lose their ability to become creative and innovative. When Germany attacked France, the French were rigidly stuck in the Maginot Line with their guns immobilized, facing one direction. It was too late for them to redesign their strategic form, and the Germans went right around them and conquered France in World War II. However, the French underground resistance emerged over time as a powerful new formative design to combat the Germans.

Threat can stimulate and challenge innovations in cultural motifs if time, resourcefulness, and capacity for multiple formativeness are already potentially available. When the Japanese attacked America on December 7,

1941, the Pearl Harbor tragedy became a rallying point, mobilizing innovation and challenging America to activate its latent industrial might. Yet, this was possible only because the capacity to develop multiple formative designs had already been nurtured and developed years before Pearl Harbor ever occurred. Had America's formativeness not been honed and pruned, rigid fundamental responses would have resulted and we might all be speaking another language in addition to English.

The collapse of formativeness in the cultural personality is most likely to happen in underdeveloped countries going from despot regimes toward communist or socialist government systems. The principles and symbols of a culture and country become rigidly and literally interpreted. The former Soviet Union espoused a communist government that supposedly would eliminate classism and the czar regime. It succeeded in reducing the vast population into one class of people repressed and imprisoned under totalitarianism. It had the seeds of its own destruction because it self-limited creative innovations of unique formativeness within its own system. The iron curtain ultimately meant curtains for the Soviet Union.

The horrifying tragic events of 9/11 are the terrifying results of Islamic fundamentalism. They are symptomatic of a larger deficit of formativeness in Arabic and Persian cultures. The constricted and fixated effects of limited formativeness will be more fully explored in future chapters. For now, it is important to note that a culture experiencing a threatening and intimidating presence of encroaching cultural life-forms needs to have developed a sense of its own formative constitution. It is lacking an integrated identity, as do many underdeveloped countries in the East. The threat of Western civilization's cultural motifs looms increasingly immense. Globalization continues to shrink an already condensed world into a greater and greater density of interaction.

Chaos theory has depicted that a butterfly batting its wings in Africa can contribute to a flood halfway across the world. The interconnectedness of countries and their cultures around the world makes global influence inescapable. What with the World Trade Organization, the International Monetary Fund, and interdependent financial markets, global influence increasingly alters and is altered by cultural formative motifs. The proliferation of cultural motifs is manifest in the shifting value of various currencies, adopted ideologies, and even the battle for whose God is the real God.

The cold war was essentially a war in peacetime over the combative proliferation of socialistic communism versus Western democratic capitalism. The outcome was determined by which culture was capable of generating the greater degree of unique and diverse formativeness aligned with its own core principles. For example, the U.S. economy expanded through diverse markets whereas the Soviet Union's collapsed because its ideology prevented diversity and pluralism. The crushing financial expense of the arms race (actually the rate of productivity) was the final straw that broke (literally—the Soviet Union went broke) their motif's back.

Unique formative motifs require freedom, open interaction, and diversity to prosper. This is the nature of the expanding universe that has infinite formativeness. Any culture that aligns itself with such an expansive and richly interactive universe will proliferate its unique, cultural motifs.

America has such vast capacities for multifaceted formativeness of motifs that its proliferation in both war and peace seems endless. However, this could also have been said for the Roman Empire during its rise and before its fall hundreds of years after its inception. The moment that a culture begins to rest on its magnificent laurels and lives off of its own rich history, the seeds of formative destruction are sewn.

The current war on terrorism invokes a unique, formative innovation of American principles. It has now included the world of civilized countries united together in a massive ideological, as well as military, war to combat the common enemy of terrorism. Actually, this alignment with such a global coalition is what might be expected from America, a country that specializes in cultural pluralism. The tragedy of 9/11 awakened the slumbering, self-indulgence of a country taking itself for granted, unprotected, and living in Disneyland. There were warnings of terrorists' threats in 1997 and 1998 (from China, Israel, and others). At that time, the U.S. government was too busy developing a case against President Bill Clinton to pay attention to what was going on in the world beyond Washington, D.C. Had the Federal Bureau of Investigation, the Central Intelligence Agency, and Congress been as obsessed with detecting terrorism and threats to the United States (connecting the dots) as they were with connecting Clinton to Monica Lewinsky (they could connect one dot on a dress to the president), we all might feel safer today. While the rest of the world has struggled with home-front terrorism (e.g., England, France, the Middle East, Russia, and Japan), America has been self-absorbed in its own vast materialistic bubble oblivious to external threats of terror. We have simply assumed somebody else will take care of the rest of the world terrorism as we are safely isolated on either side by two gigantic bodies of water. Yet, these thousands of miles of ocean are appropriately called ponds as they can be traversed by sophisticated commercial jets in a matter of hours.

The world indeed has shrunken to a virtual reality of information processing through an internal net of e-mails, Web sites, and digital satellite communications. The interactive war of formative motifs rages more fiercely now than in any special forces military action. Competing life-forms, ideologies, languages, cultural values, and currencies are all interfacing, enriching, and at times encroaching on one another. The war and peace of formative proliferation of unique cultural motifs has never been more fiercely competitive.

The collision of Western culture, known as McWorld, with Eastern civilization was inevitable. The potential enrichment of Arabic and Persian countries from such exchanges is currently outweighed by the threatening consumptive power of Western motifs. Whether intentional or simply by happenstance, America and its allies have been characterized as a gorilla, though benign, in a crystal shop. Our very size and sophistication are daunting to an Eastern culture that still fights military wars with other countries' hand-me-down hardware, cavalry charges, and wanna-be nuclear powers.

The attack on America's World Trade Center allegedly by Islamic fundamentalists using our own planes against us is pathetically their best perverted effort. Instead of building on the developmental needs of their own cultural motifs, these fundamentalists chose instead to create a horrific, perverted form of, literally, using America's achievements against itself (e.g., our commercial airliners as weapons of our own destruction). Yet, it's because of their lack of formative motifs that these fundamentalists seem so intent on attacking the infidels of the West. They have made a relatively small contribution in cultural achievements and sophistication. As a consequence of low-level formative development in their own Islamic cultural motifs, they have had precious few resources from which to draw. Ironically, they are endowed with millions of dollars from worldwide resources (Saudi Arabia, pseudocharities, etc.). Yet, they demonstrate a poverty of cultural, industrial, and spiritual development that falls short of a higher realm. As a result, they wage war at an impoverished level of mindless self-nihilism. Deficient in any real world formativeness, these terrorists engage in a version of war of the gods that is a twisted manifestation of pseudocultural motifs (e.g., the vision of 72 virgins and a litany of their nobility).

What I find curious about all this as a clinical psychologist is that these noble knights of the East are in a porn shop in Florida indulging their sexual fantasies only days before their nihilistic rampage into the World Trade

Center. Were they sexually frustrated (I'll bet Sigmund Freud would have a field day with this), deprived men projecting their lewd, sexual desires on the infidels of the West whose porn shops they frequented? Do they see Westerners as infidels because their own culture lacks the formative development of their own motifs, preventing them from having access to what they may envy and thus harbor resentment toward the West? (Would Freud suggest maybe "penis envy" for Osama bin Laden?) One can only hypothesize. One piece is for certain. Formativeness is essential for life-forms and cultural motifs to survive and thrive. John Milton wrote in his famous poem *Paradise Lost* that he would rather be a ruler in hell than a mere angel in heaven. The hellish motifs of the Taliban and Islamic fundamentalists seem to have a frightening resonance to the egotistical narcissism expressed in Milton's poem.

The seeds of terrorism are planted in the fertile stagnation of a cultural fixation. When the cultural growth of motif stagnates, the seeds of a cancerous growth are planted. The advent of globalization forces diverse cultures (West, East, American, European, Arabic, etc.) into close contact. When well-formed cultures of advanced countries interface with those of less formed (underdeveloped) countries, there are increased risks that such encounters can be seen as threatening and intimidating. Curiously enough, intensification of terrorist activities began to increase in the early 1990s, which was a time of increasing prosperity in the West and movement toward globalization. Ironically, there were in the United States increasing numbers of disaffected citizens disenfranchised from this prosperity who began to turn to Islamic fundamentalism. (What is American jihad?) It was also a time of the bombing of the World Trade Center, unrest in Somalia, and increasing radicalization in Islamic fringe elements. The West (the United States and Europe to some extent) was perceived as siding with Israel, displacing the Palestinians, and occupying Arab countries (Kuwait and Iraq in the Gulf War) while presenting a culture devoid of spirituality (i.e., materialistic capitalism).

When diverse cultures press up against one another (as in tectonic plates of the Earth grinding their edges upon one another, creating faults like the San Andreas in California), intense pressures are created. Witness the effects of globalization on countries like France and their radicalization of Jean-Marie Le Pen! The recent presidential election in France contrasted the current liberal incumbent Jacques Chirac with the hard-right conservatism of his challenger Le Pen. The latter represented an extreme pro-France position that invoked ultranationalism, a return to ethnic prejudices almost to Nazilike proportions, and a focus on harsh boundary contrasts between returning to traditional France versus a more modernized, open-ended cultural version.

While he was defeated by Chirac, Le Pen did garnish almost a third of the vote. Such politics reflect a growing trend in even the most liberal of European countries of a growing anxiety and caution of losing cultural and national identity and integrity to a perceived potential consumption by international globalization. Examples of such regressive tendencies are a growing angst with citizens who are of nontraditional European dissent (e.g., Arabs, blacks, and Asians). There are even regressive tendencies of growing prejudice toward Jews by assaulting their synagogues and increasingly blaming them for the Mideast conflict.

European countries like England are also experiencing unrest with their citizens of other ethnic origins. There is growing unrest and discontent among blacks in England regarding employment opportunities and the potential for discrimination. Even Western countries like England and France are becoming increasingly anxious, protective, and intolerant of foreigners (even naturalized citizens) appearing to take jobs away from those native or true citizens (which usually means the same culture, skin color, language pattern, or ancestral origin of birth). Threats to one's survival may take many forms. When Abraham Maslow (1968) established his hierarchy of need levels from survival to self-actualization, he recognized the regressive tendencies of fixation and stagnation. Threats to lower-level needs of physical safety, security, and belonging could impair and thwart growth and expansion of one's identity and self (or cultural) actualization. If such threats can occur in Westernized European countries (which the Islamic East has labeled infidels), imagine the magnitude of catastrophe such globalization can have on the markedly different and diverse cultures of the East.

Terrorist groups such as Al Qaeda and Hamas are indirectly supported by Muslim countries. Saudi Arabia, Libya, and Iraq are countries from which terrorist groups draw enormous financial support. The general populace of Muslim countries appears to be sympathetic to the causes of these groups, if not their tactics. The growing globalization of world economy, technology, and marketing has intensified the cultural collision of which lifestyles, values, and civilization will predominate. The emerging economic world market has reflected values of Western culture and civilization, primarily American values and democratic principles.

To many Muslim countries, which are underdeveloped and resistant to incorporating external ways of life from other cultures, this smacks of a cultural crisis of enormous proportion. Islamic principles prescribe very specific rules and rituals that are embodied in the day-to-day Muslim lifestyle. The garb of Islamic women, their relationship to men, and how the family operates in a highly loyalistic and high priority profile (e.g., Muslim children are taught to place the family's needs vastly ahead of their own individual ones) are just a few of the ways Islamic religion and lifestyles merge. Islamic indoctrination of loyalty extends toward noncritical acceptance of totalitarian regimes (e.g., the Saudi family is perceived as gods having lineage to Allah).

The onset of the Western entrepreneurial emphasis of materialistic achievement and capitalistic gain in this life (not the next world of life after death) juxtapose cultural personalities and religious worship to fissionable proportions. The seeds of terrorism reflect the Muslim world's stressor response to the imposition of global markets that threaten to tear at their very fabric of culture, religion, and identity.

Recently (Williams, 2003), President Bush admonished the Palestine Liberation Organization that Yasser Arafat must go as its leader as well as terrorism before a Palestinian state could be established. He called for elections to choose a new leader. While the merits of Arafat have little regard, many Palestinians perceive this as another sign of America— the only superpower left in the world—imposing on their conditions for how to run their lives. Some columnists even in America have referred to this more as a form of colonialism that could easily be construed as imperialism.

It is important to note Christianity and Islam both believe in monotheism. While this would seem to serve as a basis of identification and collaboration, there is something called operational definition that rears its unpleasant head. An operational definition seeks to define a construct, abstraction, or term into a specific, observable, behavioral expression. As has been previously noted, the Islamic religion has a literal, rigidly defined structure informing Muslims how to act, what to wear, and what to prioritize. Their operational definition is God (e.g., Allah) is in concrete, literal terms (e.g., Allah is Holy land or Holy cave and, Holy cow, we will die for this piece of land because "it" is Allah). Christianity in the West has been diluted as far as ritual, tradition, and priorities of lifestyle are concerned, such that an American Christian can make a six-digit income, enjoy premarital sexual encounters at will, blow off family to pursue his or her own needs and desires, and still be able to die and go to heaven. Such a perception of Muslims regarding Western Christianity understands that there is only room for one God that is monotheistic and, because the God of the

West is characterized as one of the infidels, is it any wonder there may be a sense of a growing showdown. There is room for only one God—the one of the West or the one of the East. Sounds a little like what Dorothy ran into in *The Wizard of Oz*!

While not all Muslims and Christians have such strict and rigid perceptions of one another, enough do to sanction and justify fear and anxiety of what will happen when their cultural worlds congeal. Globalization is accelerating such collisions without assisting cultures in learning and emerging to differentiate their motifs in ways that can successfully interact with one another.

In the next chapter, I will explore the effects of cultural boundary collisions, violations, and intensification of cultural impositions. The implications of reified cultural motifs with rigid operational definitions will be explored as contributions toward the growing cancerous spread of terrorism worldwide. Terrorism in this vein will be seen as a counterpositional, a destructive force emerging from the critical impasse of stunted growth of immature cultural motifs.

Chapter 3

ISLAMIC FUNDAMENTALISM AND CULTURAL SHOCK: THE CANCER BEGINS

The tremendous friction and potentiated energy created as tectonic plates of juxtaposing cultures demand simultaneous occupation can be viewed in conflicts of the Mideast and Kashmir. The cauldron of conflict between the Palestinians and Israel has been raging at murderous levels for over a half century. The recent rash of suicide bombings Israel has suffered at the hands of the Palestinians has been countered by Israeli military invasions of Palestinian territories. This endless cycle of violence continues to escalate with each transgression. The sequences of terrorist attacks become mutually self-justifying from each culture's vantage point as the tragedy of mutual bloodshed continues to inflict its gruesome toll of lives. These sequences are fueled by intensely charged emotions (e.g., grief, hate, and revenge) exerting regressive effects. The results are impaired rationale and wisdom of informative interventions.

The irony of the Mideast conflict is that the Jewish and Arabic cultures are actually derived from the same family of origin. That is, their cultural history was born from a common ancestry of the 12 Semitic tribes in biblical times. Nothing is so violent as warring conflict between members of the same family. Witness the brutality and bloodshed of the American Civil War. The closer in similarity and proximity siblings are, the less room, space, and time they have to express and be themselves. It's akin to two gunfighters in the old West; there is room at the top for only one. The intrafamilial conflict of children disputing which of a deceased parent's belonging each will have creates an either-or, win-lose context. Who will get dad's pocket watch? Who should have what property can create intense ownership and territorial conflicts at a time of great loss of a loved one and home.

Indeed, both Israelis and the Palestinians have suffered unbelievable losses and grievances. Both believe that there is room in their occupied homeland for only one, and both contest territorial rites (protests grounded in rigid, operational definitions of God and Allah) for the loss of their ancestral homeland. They are indeed warring orphans of displaced homelands with no sense of how to interface their unique cultural identities of motif. There is a reification of each culture's way of life as written in concrete. While traditions are precious, grieving cultures, like siblings, become hard and recalcitrant about what must be there for them to feel at home. Therein lies the intractable position of insisting on whose cultural identity of motif will persist in a life and death struggle. There is no interchange of cultural motifs between the Palestinians and Israelis when terrorist attacks harden hearts and prevent healing of previous wounds of loss.

The similarity of both cultural heritages fosters a magnification of the subtle distinctions to become glaring distortions. For example, the Koran's and the Bible's Old Testament on the surface appear completely different. Yet, they both embody the appearance of an omnipotent deity to a representative man-being who becomes an earthly spiritual leader of that culture. God appears to Moses through the burning bush on a mountaintop, instructing him in the Ten Commandments. The angel Gabriel appears to Muhammad in an equally secluded place of a cave from whence the Koran is written. Both Allah and Yahweh are monotheistic.

Yet, like branches of a tree where one veers to the east and the other to the west, the Jewish and Arabic cultures rooted in the family of the 12 Semitic tribes develop derivatives with unique, artistic motifs. The loss of their roots has hardened and reified their cultural formativeness of motifs into a gruesome life and death struggle. The stirring of the pot of Islamic fundamentalists has shocked each culture's heartfelt motif into stone upon which no new seeds of fruition and peaceful coexistence can grow.

The common heritage of Jewish and Palestinian cultures reveals itself in the fundamental roles of their religions. The Arabic culture focuses not of sovereignty or national identity but rather on identifying itself as part of a religious community transcending any arbitrary physical, geographic boundary. They are Muslims not Saudis or Palestinians. Their Islamic religion is the fundamental basis of their sovereign identity wherever they are.

They do not need a country in this sense to have a fundamental state of being (which is a Muslim). The spirituality of this state of being can be obscured in rigid, operational definitions of God. In some ways, this reflects the polarizations of all or nothing rootlessness (e.g., only this Holy Land is our home and no other can be). The nomadic nature is part of the tribal basis of the 12 Semitic tribes from which both cultures arose.

After the horrifying Holocaust of 6 million Jews slaughtered by Nazi Germany, the Jewish culture understandably wanted to make a home for itself. The establishment of the Jewish state of Israel was a derivational shift in their nomadic tribal motif of wandering throughout the world bound by culture, but unbound by landmass. The occupation of land in the Mideast was based on the fundamental religious principle that this was their ancestral Holy Land. It belonged to them because it was the God-given homeland of the nation of Israel.

In this formative derivation, the nomadic tribe of Israel had returned to its home at its Holy "Landmass." Here, religion now serves as the fundamental criterion to fight for and occupy what was always theirs by religious rights of passage. Such a derivational motif has challenged the Palestinian Arabs in that they cannot continue to be nomadic wanderers as the now concretized religious nation state of Israel prevents them from wandering into this new domain. This now challenges the Palestinians to develop their own derivational motif of defining their own geographical nation-state as they cannot not plant their own roots and concretize this same land as their Holy Land of Islam.

The fundamentalist conversion of religious constructs into physical objects, geographic areas, and occupied territories automatically reifies and fixates any further formativeness of their cultural motif's evolutionary development. Here we see both cultures reify and literalize their sacred, religious principles and beliefs, delimiting them into written-in-concrete commandments of how to honor their God. Ironically, they both break the first commandments of their religions in worshiping idols, false gods, and arbitrarily casting God's land as their idealized (idolized) Holy Land, which justifies the slaughter of countless human beings.

The present leaders of the Jewish and Palestinian cultures in the Mideast are Ariel Sharon and Yasser Arafat. Both are aggressive combatants preferring to strike first and ask questions later. Coupled with the radicalization of Islamic fundamentalism, the conditions are ripe for raging conflict, terrorism, and endless escalations of bloodshed. It is this concretization of motifs (in this case, religious beliefs and constructs being given literal cast-in-stone fixations) in fixed fundamental set forms of a physical reality that creates such all or nothing, life and death conflicts.

A similar kind of fundamentalist focus operates in the Pakistan and India conflict of Kashmir. As in the Mideast conflict, each country believes that its identity and honor are imbued in the Kashmir region. There are those in Pakistan who see this as a jihad, or holy war, as the Indian-controlled side of Kashmir is heavily Muslim. With a 40 percent literacy rate in Pakistan, the loss of Bangladesh in 1971 to India, and high-infant mortality rates, this is a breeding ground for terrorism and show-down politics. India seeks to establish its secular nature, yet behaves in a do-or-die, fundamentalistic recalcitrance, rigging Kashmir elections to maintain control. The fact that both have nuclear weapons bespeaks the ultimate terror.

The juxtaposition of abrasive, fixated motifs emerging in such boundary conflicts as in the Mideast and Kashmir is instructive of the encroaching impact of globalization. Such juxtapositions inflamed by a globalization insensitive to cultural motifs become the breeding ground for the seeds of terrorism.

SURVIVING GLOBALIZATION

Globalization challenges countries to learn how to operate and rise to the occasion of participating in international commerce and free trade. Globalization portrays the world market as open and available to all countries, large and small, from the technologically advanced to those in the third world. Yet, some countries are in a much better position to benefit and profit from international free trade than others.

Globalization requires the capacity to engage in highly competitive, capitalistic markets. This reflects and favors capitalistic values of Western countries, most notably America. As previously described, the powerful presence of American capitalism in the world (especially as it is the world's lone superpower) has been characterized somewhat euphemistically as McWorld. Obviously playing off the international corporation of McDonald's, it is no joke that this American corporation has proliferated itself into over 120 countries of the world. The international impact of such expansive corporate enterprises has, for countries of noncapitalistic origins, presented an intimidating and enormous incursion into their economies and cultural customs.

The economic and cultural shock of globalization can be better grasped by appreciating the historical perspective. In the 1500s, the Muslim world had, up to that point, been a hotbed of learning, scholarship, and sophistication. Up to the 1500s, Islamic culture spread throughout Europe, Asia, and Africa (DeSousa, 2002). Muslim and Arabic trade transpired with India and the Far East. The Islamic culture had established uniform laws and a sophisticated civilization. It built fabulous cities such as Baghdad, Damascus, Cairo, Istanbul, Seville, and Granada. It developed rich forms of architecture and literary and cultural splendor that surpassed current levels of European development. There were great men of learning such as Ibn Sīna (Avicenna), Ibn Rushd (Averroës), Ibn Khaldūn, al-Ghazali. Such men translated and preserved Greco-Roman literary works and espoused critiques and corrections regarding Western writings such as Galileo's observations in astronomy. Muslims perceived those in the West as living in the dark ages, ignorant, impoverished, apathetic, and unintelligent. It is the precise criticisms of the West that Westerners now have of Muslims.

By the 1500s, Western countries began to exert efforts to emerge from their dark ages. They emerged in dominance since that time because they were willing to draw upon the advancements and creations of diverse cultures (DeSousa, 2001). Western countries such as England pursued other countries' resources, such as gunpowder from China, and refined it into advancements in waging modern-day warfare. They explored and gathered the best resources, such as porcelain, silk, embroidery from China. They studied and refined various systems of government and centers of learning from the East into Western modes of living.

The West continued to absorb ideas and creative inventions from other cultures, such as the printing press and the compass. From these, the Bible was printed and naval navigation was now possible. While the West was expanding, growing, and becoming enlightened, the Islamic culture became entrenched into the position that it had nothing to learn from those "stupid, ill-refined beasts" of the West (DeSousa, 2001). The tragedy of such a cultural blockage was that periods such as the Renaissance came and went, and Western democracies emerged with new inventions and advancements of their own, without any recognition and benefit to the East.

The Islamic position that there was nothing to learn outside of their religion (which means their cultural way of life) contributed to stagnation and a role reversal of advancement with the West. As centuries would pass, it would be the Muslims being cast as the uneducated and ill refined. It is also important to grasp that the Islamic religion has a very different set of constructs for the structure of universe than the Greeks and the West. The

Muslim writer Al-Ghaohi (DeSousa, 2001) denies the Greek version of the universe and how it operates. The Greeks presumed laws of the universe that were accessible to human understanding and a reasoning that could be expressed in mathematical principles. To the Muslims, the universe was incoherent when framed in philosophical logic and reasoning. Rather, the Islamic religion directs that it is Allah who intervenes at every single moment and that all events can only be understood as caused by Allah. The Muslim version has an enchanted universe moved by spirits, which defy human logic and reason. Such a version also challenges the idea of linear progress and development. While the West, and especially American mentality, espouses that everyone and everything can grow, develop, and make progress to a better life in the future, the Muslim culture's views are just the opposite. To the Muslims, the past is the age of perfection (the golden age of harmony with Allah) and that, while there are patterns that exist today of that perfect universe, these are degenerative and do not measure up to what once was the universe according to Allah.

There are vastly different constructs between East and West. In a world of globalization and capitalistic markets, progress is the West's most important product. Cultures like the East's, whose very religion restructures the universe as essentially unchangeable, and what's more not in need of change (How can one improve on Allah's perfect universe?), will be at a severe disadvantage to handle such a world configuration. Is it any wonder that the West is viewed as infidels to the East because they would dare to "improve" on the perfect harmony of Allah's universe? This is not so hard to understand if one recalls that in America, there continues to be a major controversy between Darwinian evolutionists, which is scientific and logic based, and creationists, who are literal believers that God created man in his image, not from a monkey's and that this was done within the last 6,000 years, which defies scientific logic and reason.

The difference between the West and the East is that in the West, there is room for diversity in viewpoints. In the East, this religious viewpoint of Islam is the viewpoint of reality and the way things literally are. Religion and reality are of one union.

IMPACT OF GLOBALIZATION

The adverse effects of globalization affect other cultures in addition to the Islamic culture. French president Chirac expressed concern that globalization is not making life better for those most in need of promised benefits. Russia and China reversed their relative economic strengths from the beginning to the end of the 1990s (China had gained over Russia). Russia had only 60 percent gross national product by the end of the 1990s after it had transitioned into international economic institutions (Stiglitz, 2002). China prospered comparatively by designing its own institutions separately. In cultures that are ill prepared or whose fundamental ways of life (motifs) are incompatible with the present globalization design structure (capitalism), inequities and unfairness can result. Instead of feeling potent, enriched, and enhanced, such cultures may feel violated, oppressed, and juxtaposed against a life and death struggle.

It is here that globalization can actually and unwittingly foster stagnation and paralysis in diverse cultures ill equipped to compete in world markets. Pressed into cultural and economic corners with their backs against the wall, radical fundamentalist regressions can be seeded. In this way, global movements that impose one principle mode or motif of operation serve to unwittingly germinate seeds of discontent. There can become the seeds of terrorism that begin to grow and spread like a cancer.

The radical, fundamentalistic movements are germinating in a variety of sectors in the world. While the obvious violent extremes have emerged in the Mideast, many other areas of the world are now susceptible to such literal, recalcitrant extremes.

In historically open and liberal cultures such as those of France and England, conservative fundamentalist movements have surfaced. There are growing polarizations of all or nothing, good and bad class distinctions of intolerance as witnessed by increasing sentiments of anti-Semitism. When cultural motifs are pressed up against one another without being encouraged and allowed to discover and explore their unique deviational way of interrelating, violent eruptions can emerge. Cultures cannot live and synergistically interrelate in multifaceted ways when their borders are mutually exclusive. Such are the consequences of enmeshed boundary violations. Cultures, like people, may experience trauma and acting out.

In the next chapter, the blatant manifestation of such fundamentalist tendencies will be illustrated, related to the events of 9/11. The intolerant, win-lose style of territorial occupation and globalized market imposition can propagate conflict and a regression to terrorist strategies for survival. For cultural motifs to synergize and interrelate, there needs to be free-flowing exchange and mutual growth. Imposition of a predominant mode of cultural motif interferes with the evolution of cultural motifs. Without such evolution between and amongst motifs, there will be no deriving of mutual modes of interrelating.

Cultural motifs need to evolve into derivational forms and unique multifacetedness or they will become stagnant and fixate. They are not unlike children who need to be allowed to incorporate parts of what they received from both mother and father, synthesizing a unique hybrid of selfhood, their own derivational motif. When children are traumatized, they become fixated and stuck in their development. They can then become a real terror. It is one thing for a child to act out but it is another thing for this to be an adult who can inflict devastation and destruction on vast numbers of people. Such rigidity and fixation prevent genuine growth of derivational motifs between and within cultures and serve to seed the idea that survival can now only occur by becoming a real terrorist. Such is the substance of what follows.

Chapter 4

ENTRANCEMENT, TERRORISM, AND JIHAD: THE MALIGNANT HOLY WAR

The shock and horrific tragedy America endured on 9/11 has ignited a vast range of intense emotions, trauma, and disbelief. This stunning act of terrorism has wounded, outraged, and baffled many as to its sanity and purpose. Television talk show host David Letterman (Tucker, 2001) spoke to a bewildered nation when his show resumed broadcasting by asking the question that struck at the core of all America and the civilized world: "If you live to be 1,000 years old...will that [9/11] make any goddamn sense?" In this chapter, I will explore possible answers to this question.

Four planes were hijacked—two crashing into the World Trade Center, one into the Pentagon, and the fourth on an open field in Pennsylvania. The ringleader of the 19 terrorists aboard the four planes was Mohammed Atta (Cloud, 2001). He was a 33-year-old, well-educated Egyptian, considered shy and nonviolent as a youth. He was fluent in three languages, held graduate degrees, and had been raised by a strict father. Those who knew him would never have predicted such behavior on his part. It was as if the terrorist leader were a different person from the man his family and friends had once known.

Contributing to the shock, trauma, and emerging confusion about these terrorists and their horrific acts were letters with the same message found in Atta's luggage and in a hijacker's car as well as in the debris of crashed United Airlines Flight 93. A partial excerpt translated from Arabic is as follows:

Purify your heart and forget something called life, for the time of play is gone and the time of truth has come.... God will absolve you of your sins, and be assured that it will be only moments and then you will attain the ultimate and greatest reward....

Let each find his blade for the prey to be slaughtered.... As soon as you put your feet in and before you enter [the plane] start praying and realize that this is a battle for the sake of God, and when you sit in your seat say these prayers that we had mentioned before. When the plane starts moving, then you are traveling toward God and what a blessing that travel is. (Cloud, 2001)

In addition to such a cryptic or obtusely coded message, Atta had been described as cold and unemotional and is pictured with a staring expression; blank and far-off in focus as if in a state of fixation. Atta was an Islamic fundamentalist who was rigidly devout in the very literal, concrete, and specific practices of the Koran. He and his sect thoroughly ascribed to the ancient teachings of Muhammad advocating the jihad or holy war against the infidels or non-Islamic believers (Cloud, 2001).

Though the Islamic religion is one that advocates love and peace, the fundamentalists have selectively concentrated their attention on a strict segment of the Koran ignoring the symbolic, larger context of its true meaning and purpose (Bloom, 1995).

The mastermind behind the tragedy of September 11 is Osama bin Laden. His Al Qaeda terrorist organization has a weblike, worldwide network of self-organizing cells—or autonomous subgroups—of terrorists (Elliott, 2001). Bin Laden hides away in a labyrinth of underground caves and has a stoic, stonelike stare and exhibits an almost effeminate quality. It seems that the only joy he has is in the slaughter of his prey (as depicted in a videotape aired on December 16, 2001). With his fixed stare and shy, reticent demeanor, he seems to have similar characteristics to Mohammed Atta.

Bin Laden was born and raised as the only son of a Syrian mother. Though he is one of many sons to his Saudi Arabian father, he has been isolated and estranged from this prosperous family. While bin Laden enjoys enormous wealth (his Al Qaeda organization receives $300 million from various sources), he has been cast out by Saudi Arabia and Sudan (Riyadh, 2001). Afghanistan was the only country that offered him an enclave for terrorist training, and he joined forces there with the Taliban.

Islamic fundamentalists and their extremist beliefs are frequently characterized by what is essentially an altered state of consciousness, disconnected and out of sync with a more normal perception of reality. This particular kind of altered state is known as entrancement and can have devastating implications. It holds incredible power over human behavior if not mastered. For the psychopathic personality (Douglas, 1995; Egger, 1984; MacCulloch, Snowden, Wood, & Mills, 1983; Prentky, Burgess, & Carter, 1986; Schlesinger & Revitch, 1980), entrancement becomes a powerful force in manipulating and directing violent and destructive behavior. Further exploration of the nature of altered states and the development of entrancement is required.

ALTERED STATES AND HYPNOSIS

Arnold Ludwig (1966) coined the term altered state of consciousness (ASC). He used the following definition:

Any mental state(s), induced by various physiological, psychological or pharmacological maneuvers or agents, which can be recognized subjectively by the individual himself (or by an objective observer of the individual) as representing sufficient deviation in subjective experience or psychological functioning from certain general norms for that individual during alert, waking consciousness. (p. 167)

Ludwig is suggesting that altered states be defined in terns of an individual's subjective experience and altered psychological function. These states result from changes in sensory experiences (sights, images, smells, unique sounds, tastes, feelings, and so forth). Changes in altered states can also result from various physical activities (a runner's high), focused vigilance (intensely looking out for danger or a special loved one), and physiological alterations (alcohol- or drug-induced states). Hypnotic states are altered states that create changes in how individuals perceive themselves and their way of dealing with outer surroundings. The absorption and engrossment in what and how the individual is perceiving and experiencing are greatly increased compared with these functions in the awakened individual.

For example, hypnotized individuals can be intensely absorbed in dreams or hallucinations of people who aren't really there, or numbed to painful dental procedures. This feature can enable terrorists to hallucinate going to heaven and to be numb to the pain of a plane crash. The sense of time is greatly distorted—a five-minute childhood memory can subjectively be perceived to last all day or a 20-minute plane ride can seem like an eternity. Individuals in these states are quite resistant to outside interruptions and distractions. A special feature of hypnotic states is that it takes energy and applied attention to induce, alter, and change states. This is an important dynamic principle of hypnosis and has significant implications for future work in releasing these bonds.

The definition of hypnosis is a special state of altered consciousness wherein select capacities are emphasized while others fade into the background. Nine out of ten people can be hypnotized. Hypnosis presents an appropriate metaphor and framework for understanding terrorist relationships. In hypnosis, there is a powerful fixation, absorption, and induction of a trancelike phenomenon. It requires people to have their conscious, critical faculties suspended as they become more and more absorbed into their personal experiences. This state has a very powerful, sensory-concentrated nature. The qualities of the hypnotic experience parallel bonding in terrorist relationships. However, to fully understand this parallel, it is essential to fully grasp the essence of the hypnotic experience.

In understanding the rationale and position of using hypnosis as a framework or structure for understanding terrorist bonding, it is important to realize that these relationships have the qualities and elements of a regressive sense of loss of control, which diffuses the sense of self. What this means is that partners feel hopeless and helpless as they intertwine in an intense, angry, isolated, and unrewarding pursuit of their hypnotic, childlike fantasies. Each person experiences mutual disappointment, frustration, and aggravation with his or her life situation as his or her entrancement deepens (Feeney, 1999). As entrancement serves only to intensify regressive, childlike demands while preventing constructive, responsible actions to correct the terrorist's miserable life conditions, the rage of dissatisfaction and deprivation only increases. The self-defeating and perpetuating loop creates an infinite regression as terrorists become even more entrenched in the very entrancements that blind them to what they can really do to change their impoverished life conditions.

Hypnosis has a unique parallel to that type of paradigm or framework in the sense that hypnosis involves getting the individual's permission, piquing his or her interest, and narrowing his or her attention. It involves a turning inward and, at times, regressing or moving forward in time. It involves a quality of selective concentration where individuals become intensely absorbed, focused, and fixated to the extent that they lose an outer sense of a generalized reality orientation.

Partners in terrorism perceive qualities in each other that seem charismatic. Such qualities may be physical features (body shape) or personality traits (enthusiasm, extroversion), which merge together in ways that fixate (narrowing of attention) partners on their perfect fantasy (which involves selective concentration). Inner, compulsive feelings (turning inward) to possess each other emerge. Partners lose track of time and daily agendas (a loss of generalized orientation). Such an encounter could be construed as a form of hypnotically induced hallucination. Hypnotized subjects can positively hallucinate or see images of their fantasies in front of them that aren't there. It can be said that partners are in a mild trance, hallucinating their idealized fantasy onto one another. Partners in terrorism are quite oblivious to the real character within themselves due to entrancement.

Another important feature of hypnosis is that it generates two types of attentional absorption, both resistant to outside interruptions and distraction. The first type is called selective attention, which is usually good for problem solving on a specific skill level (dealing with educational concerns, weight loss, smoking cessation programs, and so forth). The other type is called expansive attention and allows a full range of stimulation and associations to be received through a stream of consciousness (witness the rush of sensations and attentional flow of riding a motorcycle at high speed or of planes flying into the World Trade Center).

It appears that selective attention will increase the intensity of the specific experience at hand (staring at a moving watch can intensify the impact on and sensation of movement in the observer as well as any suggestions given about people, places, or things). Such staring expressions can be observed on some of the faces of the terrorists (such as Atta and Zacarias Moussaoui). Expansive attention will allow increases of receptivity to a stream of consciousness of feelings and memories (hearing a favorite song can open an individual to a vast range of memories, feelings, and nostalgia). Hypnotic states can be induced through application of these various types of attention and focus.

Relaxation and hypnosis are usually associated with one another, as creating a relaxed and tranquil mind occurs through a relaxed and tranquil body. Hypnosis can occur in states of physical arousal and alertness. For example, when a car's headlights shine into the eyes of a deer standing by the side of the road, it will freeze in an alert and aroused position. It is in an altered state, yet hardly relaxed. Hypnosis can occur in both relaxed hypoarousal and tense, vigilant hyperarousal.

Hypnosis also alters our general reality orientation (GRO) (Tart, 1969). When we are driving on the highway, it is our GRO that prevents us from crossing over the white line separating lanes, even when our minds are on something else. In hypnosis, the stable internal frame of reference created by the GRO is diminished. Hypnotized individuals may have some awareness of outside sounds and sensations, like people talking or cars going by, but they are less acutely aware or responsive to their presence. They are less distracted and more focused.

In deep hypnosis in which individuals have completely relinquished their GRO, the higher cognitive functions of analysis and interpretation of here-and-now sensations are reduced. Such a reduction occurs when an individual is so attracted and absorbed by something (a great-looking car, job, house, suicide bombing, etc.) or someone (a well-shaped physique) that the individual unconsciously lowers his or her rational guard and impulse fantasies are entertained. At this point, sensory hallucinations and distortions may occur (there may be analgesic experiences where the pain of a toothache may be numbed). The loss of GRO is what Atta sought in urging the suicide bombers to remain focused and "think only of traveling to heaven" (Cloud, 2001).

Hypnosis involves dissociation, in which tranced individuals may have memories and perform acts without realizing that they are actually doing them (take the case of automatic writing where hypnotized subjects will unconsciously write out ideas and feelings but have no recognition that they are doing it or what they wrote).

Hypnosis also creates what is known as trance logic (Brown & Fromm, 1986). This refers to the ability of hypnotized individuals to put together perceptions partially based on their real-world experience mixed and intertwined with those that are based on fantasy and imagination. The resultant perspective is that such a fusion of reality and fantasy creates hallucinations and distorted thinking patterns among hypnotized individuals. Because they are in an altered state, there is extreme tolerance for contradictions and ambiguity. An example of this is the hypnotized individual believing he sees a close friend whom he hallucinates to be his mother or father. There may be distorted logic of thought. If that close friend smiles or frowns, then the individual will think that the hallucinated parent is either loving or rejecting. The trance logic of the terrorists is that the more murders of infidels there are, the more Allah will smile.

A further quality of hypnotized individuals is perceived involuntarism. Here, hypnotized individuals seem to be passively observing themselves act in ways that have no purpose. They feel as if things are being ruled by other forces. Hypnotic suggestion can create the effect that automatic eye closure is involuntary and beyond conscious control, leaving hypnotized individuals unable to open their eyes.

Yet, paradoxically, the hypnotized individual is using a strategic trance logic to achieve the goal of hypnotic eye closure by splitting his awareness. That is, as he consciously attends to a watch moving in front of him, he is distracted from awareness of how his eye concentration causes fatigue, closure, and inner associations. When this perceived involuntarism occurs during an absorbed state of a stream of consciousness, there can be vivid imagery, memories, and changes of body image (as in "I felt like an airplane and decided to fly; my nose became the shape of a bird's beak"). Trance increases the quality and sense of realism of imaginary experiences and illusions. Because hypnotized individuals reason and think with a sensory, trance logic (the feeling of being like an airplane must mean that I am one and can now act like one), they are especially prone to feeling involuntarily controlled by inner and outer stimuli and sensations. Imagine the sense of the suicide bomber who is in an altered state literally experiencing the reality of being Allah's holy warrior, involuntarily having to kill himself and thousands of others.

A key aspect of hypnosis is the special nature of the hypnotic relationship (Brown & Fromm, 1986). The increased availability of inner feelings, associations, images, and memories in hypnotized individuals begins to filter and shape the relationship with the hypnotist. A strong intensity and intimacy emerge between the hypnotist and the hypnotized individual. The vivid internal imagery and other highly personal sensations create a regressive effect. There is an infantilism where the individual experiences gratification of infantile wishes (attention, centeredness, and parental-like guidance). In addition, the fading of the GRO that results from a restriction of input from the outside world and the narrowing of range communication (the hypnotist is the only one the individual is able to contact) all creates a dependent, parent-child-like relationship with the hypnotist. It is not unlike the special relationship of a mother-child bond. The effects of such a special intense bond create powerful transference effects (transferring or shifting perception and images from past significant parental figures to the here-and-now person of the hypnotist). The skillful hypnotist can use such regressive intensity for meaningful therapeutic change. The hypnotist realizes that his or her impact on the individual can be so intense as to seem almost magical. If the "hypnotist" is a psychopath such as Osama bin Laden, imagine the manipulative and exploitative influence he can have over such entranced terrorism.

SIGNS OF HYPNOTIC TRANCE

The signs of trance involve such concepts as depth of trance or responsiveness to suggestion. For example, arm catalepsy (when the hypnotized individual discovers his or her arm is rigid) indicates a depth of trance and responsiveness to hypnotic suggestion. Many times there are no behavioral signs of trance, only that the individual subjectively feels deeply hypnotized and intensely absorbed. Yet, this same individual may not behaviorally respond because he or she is in trance. The perceptual rigidity of Islamic fundamentalists is suggestive of altered states and it would not be difficult to begin to understand them in terms of entrancement.

Hypnotized individuals usually experience or demonstrate some or all of the following signs: ideomotor phenomena (alterations in physical movements caused by thinking and imagining such as arm catalepsy) and cognitive and sensory effects (easier access to the inner world of dreams, imagery, emotions, memories, and amnesia and age regression to early childhood experiences) (Brown & Fromm, 1986).

Further signs of trance experience involve the persistent effects of posthypnotic suggestions and amnesia. Here, hypnotized individuals will be given suggestions to act or think a certain way after being awakened from the trance. They will also be given suggestions for amnesia or forgetting that such suggestions for posthypnotic behavior were ever given. For example, individuals may be given the suggestion that their understanding of conflicts and problems will become more and more clear over time after they awaken and leave the room.

Special cognitive abilities occur in trance as hypnotized individuals are capable of changing the meaning and value of words, fantasies, thoughts, and beliefs about experiences (new insights and understandings can be discovered). There can be perceptual changes in reality, illusions, hallucinations, and delusions created (factual reality can merge with fantasies, creating hallucinations, as in a real flower fantasized to be smiling; alterations in self-concept and self-esteem may be inflated or amplified by imagining self as successfully performing in school or work). Listed below are 13 criteria of signs of trance:

1. Relaxation or drowsiness
2. Responsiveness to suggestions
3. Absorption or involuntary experiencing
4. General reality orientation fading
5. Vivid imagery or hallucinations

6. Selective or expansive attention
7. Unconscious involvement
8. Access to inner sensing
9. Age regression
10. Time distortion
11. Amnesia and hyperamnesia
12. Parallel awareness
13. State-dependent learning, memory, and behavior beyond waking consciousness

ENTRANCEMENT IN HYPNOSIS

A main premise advanced is that terrorists' behavior and ways of functioning in their relationships intimately parallels similar dimensions of those in hypnotic altered states. The dimensions that are present in bonds among terrorists involve, if not require, hypnotic dynamics and forces to sustain them. The special type of altered state in such relationships is known as entrancement.

Entrancement is an alignment of matching energies and expectations at one of the deepest levels of human experience, which constitute attraction, resonance, and union between thematically similar and congruent persons (similar in thinking and believing) at many levels of their life experiences (images, feelings, characters, fantasies, chemistry, etc.). Entrancement involves suspension of critical faculties (meaning we lose our mind and surrender ourselves to some fantasy ideal way of living). It also involves selective attention filtering out incompatible information. These and many other facets suggest that the power of entrancement is hypnotic in origin. Relationship bonding between would-be terrorists and leaders can be comprehended in such a hypnotic framework.

Entrancement involves a coming together or fusion of idealized images superimposed upon action plans designed by a terrorist leader (Osama bin Laden) that match and merge with the follower's expectations (Mohammed Atta). Each person brings to the relationship ideals or images of his perfection merged into the others. Such a merger of fantasy ideals embedded into specifically designed action plans (e.g., the holy wars of the jihad against the Western infidels) unleashes incredible forces for acting out catastrophic deeds in the name of God (Allah).

Entranced relationships contribute to terrorist functioning when the terrorists are unable to progress successfully from one state to the next. They experience difficulty in releasing one section or state of their relationship growth for the next one, which would assist them in continuing their journey. It is important to note that most terrorists are not aware, or are only vaguely aware, of the extent to which hypnotic entrancements operate in their significant relationships. When in entrancement, they experience chronic problems (conflicts, verbal or physical abuse, and other struggles). It is at this level of restrictive relating that they experience the perverse twist of merged bonding. Without learning to master, understand, and gain a perspective on hypnotic entrancement, there is great risk that the nightmarish perversion of literal, fused bonding is heightened. This can be observed when intensification of entranced fantasy ideal mergers occurs. Bin Laden has portrayed himself as speaking and wearing the robe of Muhammad, whom is claimed in Islamic religion to have spoken to the angel Gabriel. Bin Laden is tall, wears a long robe, and claims to, in some ways, embody the literal, as well as figural, presence of Muhammad (who himself was in the presence of sacredness). By association, to the Islamic fundamentalist, bin Laden could easily be construed in fantasy ideal as a deity. There is almost a love affair going on between such charismatic leaders and their followers. In some ways, the bonds between and among terrorists have such addictive alterations in states of perceiving and relating to one another. The following section describes how such entranced bondings may operate.

Partners say the perfume was hypnotizing and the personality mesmerizing. These statements are not just euphemistic terms. They access the powerful fixation and self-inductive quality of their own self-hypnotic image of what smacks of beauty, aura, and charisma. Indeed partners create their own self-induced trance without knowing it.

In this self-talk, self-inducing trance begins a powerful journey into the deepest recesses of their own, unconscious minds. It is indeed an instantaneous, rapid induction. In *West Side Story,* Tony sees Maria across the dance floor, and the sudden, unexpected shock effect of that "perfect vision" entrances him into "love." The pair begins to induce a mutual spell over each other. Gazing into one another's eyes is the type of eye fixation that occurs in the beginning stage of hypnotic induction. The hypnotist says to his subject, "Let your eyes focus on some point on the wall. As you continue to stare, your eyelids could become heavy, so heavy that they may close, and you might feel more relaxed about going into trance whenever you are ready, either now or in a few moments."

This motivates and entrances, responding to the idealized person as a resonation of an individual's internal, idealized thinking and imagining, which is now activated, projected, and fused onto the other. If one senses and discovers another person with his or her own unique and mysterious qualities that match one's idealized fantasies, instant rapport and absorption can develop. Everyone has some internal construct of an idealized partner. That one becomes absorbed into one's own internalized image, and in fantasy expectations of who one projects that person to be, constitutes remarkable self-deception. Such self-deception is further enhanced when an assessment of a partner is based on physical features of the body shape and size. The fusion of body image with personality attributes matches the fantasized ideal projection as one and the same. The boundary between our inner and outer worlds has now merged into one and the same. What was perceived as fantasy is now reality to partners. While one sees a princess, the other sees a very plain-looking girl.

There is a slow but sure inductive quality between the "I" and the "other," which begin to mesh because of matching projections (misattributions). They make their entrance into that inductive quality of meshed oneness that has the quality of selective attention, seeing only the best in the "other" as our ideal partner. Just such a merger of mind-body fantasy ideal and physical presence may well occur between bin Laden and his followers. Yet, as will be seen, there is a very dark, ominous side to this love affair with terrorism.

Addictive self-induction starts when partners are perceived to possess an exotic, charismatic personality associated with selective attributes that are now entranced into that addictive image of the other. Physical, sensory, and personality characteristics that partners attributed to one another create hypnotic induction. Partners see the other person as someone who reflects a fantasy of having it all. Partners are not seen as only models of fantasy. Rather, partners experience each other as a living, breathing manifestation of fantasy come true.

Embedded within the entranced fantasy ideals that partners have of one another lie hidden elements of envy. While one partner may admire and idealize the other, that partner may also secretly wish that he or she too possessed such valued attributes. Such hidden envy for the other's attributes is highly intensified in entrancement as a result of lost self-identity boundaries.

Entrancement tends to create such paradoxical, dialectical tensions in intimate relationships. The power of the hypnotic pull is the envious absorption and consumption of what the other has, not who the other might uniquely be as a person. Entranced partners equally lose sight of their own unique characters, falling prey to the fused, paradoxical themes that permeate entranced relationships. Partners experience conflicting pulls, feeling on the one hand that they cannot live without each other, and yet on the other cannot stand to live with the other.

Entrancement encourages each partner's self-boundary toward diffusion and disintegration. Partners lose the ability to maintain a separate and distinct integrity that attributes to his or her unique characteristics. Each becomes absorbed into the other's attributes. The consequences are fear, jealousy, and a lost self.

Overidentification (partners seeing themselves in each other to the point of losing their own sense of self), plus exaggerated admiration and envy, can mean that partners develop fear of the unique qualities they so dearly love in each other. Partners' fear of intimacy is actually the fear of one's own uniqueness. Without uniqueness, there can be no intimacy. Entrancement creates the illusionary reality that intimacy is its own outcome. Romantic entrancement espouses the allure, passion, and heat of embrace. Yet, the paradox presents itself that entrancement creates the very fear and avoidance of each partner's unique qualities that are essential for intimacy. Entrancement, therefore, stands in its own way toward the path of intimate relating.

If entrancement interferes (by creating fears) with itself in the pursuit of intimacy, the resulting distortions create a reality denied. Entrancement is an illusion appearing real, forever denying a partner's fulfillment of the entrancement's false promises. Illusions induce surrendering a sense of control and authority in each other's life.

There is a rapid connection and induction characteristic in this kind of relationship. The problem in the beginning, as in all addictive relationships, is that the fantasy is expected and demanded to happen instantly. It is not seen as a journey with a desirable outcome to be nurtured and developed. It becomes a should, a must, an ought-to-happen-now. It becomes an irrationality of pressing partners into this neurotic, illusionary shape, fitting into the needs of the hypnotic pull. This results in denying both one's own self and the other person's identity.

Herein lies the true nature of the addiction. There is insistence that this fantasy be embodied in partners as a means of gratifying life fulfillment. The boundaries of inner thoughts and images become blurred and vulnerable to confused fixations. Partners attribute super powers to the other that can now supposedly change our lives.

This kind of omnipotent thinking and imaging is powerfully entrancing. It is designed to fulfill the complete induction of merging into an all-consuming, all-encompassing, larger-than-self bonding and nurturing. What is fantasized inwardly (both on a need- and idealistically based fantasy) is fused outwardly with external physical and personality attributes of our partner. There is a submergence and entrancement of inner and outer worlds fused into one. Addictive fusion through this self-induced hypnotic state begins to corrupt character.

With a suspension of critical faculties, entrancement activates mistaken beliefs stemming from distorted early childhood learning. It also engenders a suspension of volitional control, in which partners act as if they cannot help what they do. Entrancing experiences create a sense of being illusionarily taken over by the magic and wonder of this enmeshment of inner and outer worlds. It now takes on an entity all its own, so powerfully real that it now displaces commonsense logic. There is no reasoning with partners at this point.

They cannot sort out fact from fiction. Entrancement demands perfection. As quickly as times between partners can become beautiful and wondrous, they can also turn sour and stormy as rapidly as a flash flood. The slightest deviation from perfect role-playing of the ideal fantasy can result in raging jealous outbursts, accusations of betrayal, and violent attacks (verbal, emotional, or physical) against the infidels. Such are the regressive effects of entrancing relationships.

These are the kinds of disqualifications of each other's fantasy needs that begin to emerge when two partners have mutually induced a trance. They evoke turbulence in pulling apart, only to dive deeper into enmeshment. A temporary pulling apart creates a fear of loss, which causes partners a loss of balance (a key feature in increasing susceptibility to trance) and serves only to deepen the pull of entrancement. They are not deviant people. They are not sick. They are not ill. They are entranced. Very few people grow up without some painful, personally damaging experiences. Partners in these types of relationships do not necessarily qualify for psychiatric treatment in and of themselves. Partners in such relationships, if not "detranced" and genuinely awakened, will be driven to the point of frenzied emotional, spiritual, and eventual physical bankruptcy.

It is especially important to emphasize a unique factor of the idealized state. As in hypnosis, both parties begin to discover that by being in this type of relationship, they can now be someone that they always wanted to be but previously never believed or dreamed they could be. For example, one partner believed that, suddenly, he had found somebody who gave him all the love, admiration, and attention previously denied him. Such idealization reaches a peak level of entrancement that is narcissistic because of the nature of its self-centeredness. It results from a pyramid effect (a hypnotic technique) of one positive suggestion of specialness building upon another and another until partners believe they are each other's god. A hypnotized individual appears to behave involuntarily (as with arm rigidity). Yet, if the hypnotic induction suggests a kind of imagining and associating that has a goal-directed purpose (or it creates arm rigidity), this will be the outcome. Since critical faculties of judgment are suspended, this allows the hypnotized individual to function at a regressed level of immaturity, preoccupied with sensory gratification without conscious censorship or interference.

Such imaginary, associative, goal-directed strategy and regressed immaturity, with a suspension of critical faculties, operates in entrancing relationships. Entranced couples appear to act in involuntary, rigid ways, yet the imagery and strategy of their idealism creates a goal-directed outcome. In this case, it is a fixated, rigid way of treating each other so as to maintain the fantasized idealism of the relationship. It's a kind of "arm rigidity" of a fixated mind-set. This can lead to apparent, involuntary actions and reactions from each partner. Conflicts can ensue with both being surprised at how they are acting. They are not aware of an unconscious strategy and goal-fixated behavior.

It is intriguing to note that the followers of bin Laden and the Taliban in Afghanistan entranced others into their fantasy ideals and action plans not to live together but rather to "die for Allah" (Cloud, 2001). An inherent betrayal, jealousy, and envy within terrorist schemes to obliterate whomever they entrance into their web of global cells. While they advocate a holy war against the West and the infidels, it is their very own "lovers" whom they betray in this perfect world of entranced paradise. Followers like Richard Reid (who carried C-4 explosives inside his shoes on board an American Airlines transatlantic flight from Paris to Miami) are easily led because of their dysfunctional, weak, and impressionable nature (they are easily entranced).

Yet, there is something even more ominous about terrorist entrancements. The jealousy and rage they have regarding the West are also a characteristic of entrancement in which one partner sees the slightest deviation from perfection of fantasy idealism, from purity, as betrayed in itself. It is quite possible that bin Laden, the Taliban, and Al Qaeda and its network of cells are rigidly obsessed and fixated on the West as the infidels because they are also *entranced* with us. The obsession, absorption, and demand for pure perfection of fantasy ideals leave no room for deviation or difference. It is intolerable for such entranced Islamic fundamentalists to allow the West to exist. Bin Laden refers to American support of Israel, its bombing in Afghanistan, and other actions. Yet, when the United States has withdrawn from conflict in that region in the world, this has only fanned the flames of radical fervor. Therefore, it is that we exist, that we are as a shining fantasy ideal of our own perfection, with our own physical body of manifest achievements (skyscrapers, massive commercial jet airliners, abundant wealth, technological advancement, and so forth) that threatens to consume bin Laden and his kind. How can he believe and merge with his own fantasy ideals of Allah when he himself may be obsessed with annihilation by the existence of those in the West? It is not an overt act of war that threatens bin Laden. It is the covert act of his own hidden entrancement with the West that threatens his fidelity with Islamic principles. He and his fundamentalist followers are catatonically rigid and fixated, seeking to annihilate their outer fixation of the West (and all that it has achieved and what they want in their own way but do not have) by seeking the actual physical destruction of the West.

There are multiple conditions (presented in the next section) that contribute to the presence of terrorism. Entrancement fixation is both a consequence of these conditions and a causal perpetuation of their escalation. For example, one reason we may not be liked is because someone like bin Laden perceived our military power as overwhelming in the Gulf War but lacking resolve in Somalia. The consequence is an ever-skewed fixation (entrancement) by bin Laden of the West as the infidels who have vast resources (which he does not) but are empty of will (which he idealizes in his terrorism). Such consequential entrancement now perpetuates further distortions of the West as imposing, restrictive, but morally weak infidels, which further justifies bin Laden's abusive, terroristic activities. Such interactive cycles feed into bin Laden's own entrancement with us (the ultimate infidel), which is self-conflicted and intolerable for his own existence.

Bin Laden betrays himself, his ideals, and his religion, as do all of his entranced fundamentalists who idealize what they can only have in the next life. He cannot live in his fantasy world when the seeds of his own destruction lie within him. This is not unlike a married man who is supposed to love and idealize his wife, but is tempted and entranced by the beauty across the pond from where he lives. Because his own inner entrancement with the forbidden fruit is so intense, he labels her a whore, a prostitute, and says she should be eliminated. Yet, her beauty does not harm him; only his entranced vision of her threatens him from within, tempting him to betray, to be the infidel. Bin Laden's projections onto the West betray his interjections of the East—what he sees in us is what he sees in himself.

CONDITIONS OF ENTRANCEMENT

The conditions most likely to lead to terrorism simultaneously induce entrancement and are met in the Islamic fundamentalist quality of life experience. They involve environmental deprivation (of food, clothing, money, etc.), authoritarian parenting with an emphasis on strict discipline, and a limited range of choices and self-expression. In addition, there is a sense of being disenfranchised from the community and culture at large, of feeling hopeless and ineffective. Because of this restrictive range of expressions, entrancement is more likely to happen.

The Arabic and Persian countries have suffered from social, educational, and political deficits, with the masses left struggling, being ruled by totalitarian regimes. Iraq is a classic example of a country with a self-serving leader who identifies himself with a stallion, seeking his own glory and oppressing the population at large when it deviates from his path. This creates disenfranchised citizens oppressed and limited in choices and opportunities. Islamic fundamentalists recruit from such populations of disenfranchised citizens who are susceptible to their enticing and entrancing qualities. The fundamentalists offer a noble purposefulness that can be found in giving up one's life for one's culture. The children in Afghanistan were being educated by the Taliban to prepare themselves to sacrifice their lives (in suicide bombings and other acts of violence) in the future as a way to travel to God (Allah). They are taught that the sensory rewards and pleasures of this world were to come in the next life (72 virgins in heaven and so forth). In this way, their sense of hopelessness, futility, and lack of meaningfulness in this life could be manipulated to serve the Islamic fundamentalists' purpose of using them for mindless acts of violence. That is exactly what happened on September 11. That was clearly an act of mindless rage and violence that will never make any sense.

One can perceive the powerful effects of entrancement operating in Atta's message to the other terrorists. He says, "Purify your hearts and forget something called life" (Cloud, 2001). This is a powerful message to fixate on some imagined (entranced), unreal, godlike holiness and to ignore the sensory world around you while you're about to murder thousands of innocent human beings. That last part he left out. Had he inserted it, it would have awakened them into the real-world experience of a generalized reality orientation of what they were going to do to themselves, as well as to many others who never hurt them. By saying the time for play is over, he narrows their focus and fixates them on a vague delusion of doing God's work, with some ultimate reward coming in the next life. The hopelessness that Atta felt, in that he believed he could never rise to any significant position in Egypt, restricted his sense of orientation to reality in this world. He was a purist and wanted his world to be perfect. This involved eliminating all injustice and unfairness. His inner fantasy ideal of excellence in his field was so abated that he manifested his ideal into a real-world delusion that he'd rather be a "captain of a plane headed for hell than a servant in heaven." His entrancement was a ferocious and violent, perverse delusion that all of his earthly privations would be rectified in some sensory (delusional and hallucinatory) manifestation in the next life. In other words, an Earth in heaven rather than a heaven on Earth.

By using the empowering achievements of America, vis-à-vis awesome commercial airliners colliding with its symbols of financial greatness (the World Trade Center), he was able to twist and pervert his own sense of futility on this Earth into a Pyrrhic victory, "blaming the infidels" for what his own country of Egypt was actually preventing him from having. By distorting in entrancement the powerful achievements of the West as signs of evil, he was able to deny his own unacceptable desires for the very things he himself so dearly wanted, but believed he would never have. This is not unlike a lover who kills the one he loves so that, if he can't have her, no one can (because she was an evil harlot anyway—or so the distortion might go). The entrancing-like qualities of fixation, stonelike numbness, and flatness of emotion are all consistent characteristics of trancelike altered states. Judgment and critical faculties are temporarily suspended as the altered state now operates in a rigid, tunnel-like attentional focus. Trying to communicate in a critical dialogue with a terrorist in that state is like trying to play chess with someone on drugs.

The mixing of the afterlife into the delusional fixation feeds into the authoritarian higher-power distortion. When people feel helpless and ineffective, they are susceptible to such fixations and inculcations of altered power sources. Both Atta and bin Laden had restrictive and authoritarian family orientations, yet they were in one form or another ostracized, estranged and alienated from their families. In children, such fantasy ideals of nobility, importance, and significance are quite intense. Research has shown (Schlesinger & Revitch, 1980) that violent, antisocial acts occur when so-called harmless fantasy and imagination regarding sexual scenarios are no longer contained in adulthood. The being of the perpetrator can no longer be contained within the fantasy as it has lost its ability to satiate inner desires. The potential for abuse in these families is high and the displacement of violence and aggression from the self to others is to be expected as the child grows into adulthood. The preoccupation with restricting sexuality in Arabic cultures, the harsh discipline, the physical beatings, and oppressiveness all contribute to abusive childhood conditions. The sudden conversion of Atta in the mature adult years of his life, while on the surface surprising and atypical of terrorists, reflects the impact of entranced fantasization manifesting itself in real-world behaviors of violence and terror. All of this is experienced in the entranced delusion as noble, just, and holy as it is fused in the literal word of Islamic fundamentalists. To the terrorists, this is the literal word of Allah, and when Atta wrote that those terrorists on the plane were traveling to God, it was then that they were most fixated on this entranced fusion of the literal word of Allah with earthly actions, while with this fusion the terrorists were being manipulated with a cloaking of the horrific mayhem that was about to be unleashed.

Entrancement is easier to generate when there is no separation between fact and visions of the future. Islamic fundamentalism dissolves the boundary line between mastering the Koran and mastering jihad against the West. This radical form of Islam operates under delusional, or trance, logic, so that the living proof of God's validity is in the power to defeat all others.

When the United States failed to demonstrate powerful responses to Islamic attacks (Beirut bombings in 1983, the U.S. withdrawal from Somalia, the 1993 World Trade Center bombing), the fundamentalists regarded these strategic victories as religious victories. It is not unlike children saying my dad (my God) can beat up your dad (your God). Such entranced logic of politics and religion can be seen throughout history (Hitler's dream of the thousand-year Reich, Napoleon's vision of European domination, etc.).

The Islamic fundamentalists envisioned themselves as uniting the Muslim world, extending from Europe to the Philippines, and eventually throughout the world. Osama bin Laden and Mullah Omar are entranced with the vision of wearing the cloak and staff of Muhammad. In short, they see themselves as Islam's new messiahs.

There has been a syllogistic logic attached to their formative construction of God (Allah) (Krauthammer, 2001). The construction of the Islamic warrior is: My God is great and omnipotent. I am a warrior for God. Therefore, victory is mine. The caveat to this is that God is strictly and rigidly defined as a power exclusively for war, the fundamentalists' war, and nothing else. It is through this purist, self-absorbed, and ill-formed constructiveness that these fundamentalists expose their own deluded entrancement. As the United States has defeated the Taliban in Afghanistan, the Taliban's formulation that might makes right has caused the voice of the fundamentalists to grow quiet. Their illusion has been shattered. Their God is not God.

Yet, entrancement (the merger of fact and fantasy) is difficult to break. The fusion of visionary fantasy ideals of world domination with terrorist activities lives on in many terrorists' minds.

The major premise of their syllogism is that God is omnipotent. Yet, everything else that follows is a sign of their deluded entrancement. First, they assume that terrorist assaults constitute what a warrior of such a God (Allah) would do. However, the glaring severity of how delusional their entrancing state actually is occurs in their conclusion. Victory is not God's, it is the terrorists'. The entrancement is so intense that these extreme radicals terrorize their own God by claiming his or her victory (whatever that actually would be) as theirs—"victory is mine" (Cloud, 2001, pp. 64–67).

That is why they lost in Afghanistan. The awesome power of the United States was sustained by a world coalition of countries enhancing and supporting the war effort. Had this coalition not been gathered, the awesome might of the United States might have had great difficulty in delivering its overpowering forcefulness and defeating the Taliban and Al Qaeda.

The truncated view and tunnel vision of bin Laden (ironically he lives in tunnels and caves) suffers from visionary entrancements that are devoid of judgment, reality-testing, and dealing with the real needs of the Arab people. The poverty, poor education, and oppressive political condition of Arabic and Persian people need real-world assistance in this life (Zakaria, 2001). The entranced delusional altered states of Islamic fundamentalists are so busy trying to steal victory from Allah to be their victory, sending other Arabs on suicidal, entranced "travels to God," that they have forgotten what is needed in this world. The entrancement of living to die is a dangerous, delusional perversion that makes death seem more attractive than life in this world. One can only speculate what Atta would have been like if he had achieved prominence in the field that he studied at university and had had 72 virgins available to him at the same time. Would that reality serve to reorient him to a more responsible, moral, and motivated way of life in this world?

Further signs of entrancement can be seen in how the terrorists construed (or misconstrued) their design fantasy ideal of the afterlife. It is an ideal of purist qualities (that's why it is pure fantasy) where there is an absolute and pious right and an absolute and impious wrong. An uncritical attitude can be seen in Mohammed Atta. He repeated his mantralike set of instructions to himself and the others as the planes were being boarded. This set of instructions reflects a pure, unchallenged, uncritical, blind acceptance of its absolute truth and validity. It is clear from such instructions that they were to function more as a kind of informal hypnotic induction and deepening, placing their induced subjects in altered states of regression. What this means is that persons experiencing such mental states of alteration function at a cognitive awareness level of primary processing. This level involves literal, concrete acceptance. Whatever is described and depicted as being true in image or as a sensory-based experience will be accepted uncritically as being valid. When Atta described the steps that the terrorists would take on the plane, instead of stating the factual truth that they were all on a suicide mission and would collide with a skyscraper, he described how they would be "traveling to heaven, to God" (Cloud, 2001, pp. 64–67). The sensory-based experience of describing what sensations persons in such altered states will feel and what it will mean is part of their literal, uncritical, fluid acceptance of someone leading them down the path. This is not to suggest that the other terrorists were unwitting conspirators and didn't know what they were doing. It does mean that they, like Atta, were already susceptible to such intense, entrancing fantasy ideals because of the deprivation and unfulfillment in their lives.

The descriptions of what heaven will hold for them (passion, nobility, forgiveness, etc.) not only titillated their imagery and fantasy, but accessed sensory experiences not gratified in their present lives. For example, Atta and others were described as visiting a pornography shop before the tragedies were to unfold. There, they could indulge their sensory titillation of what was to be theirs in the next life. It seems curious that such soldiers of God would prepare themselves to be in the presence of eternal holiness by visiting a pornography shop. How pious and honorable is that?

The entrancement of the fantasy ideal of gaining heaven through killing people was reinforced by the literal regressive acceptance that this was the omnipotent word and will of Allah. The fusion or merger of such fantasy ideals involving terrorist activities with the infinite power of a god serves to intensify such entrancement. It is not unlike Adolph Hitler, who believed that destiny was on his side, willing him to exterminate the Jews.

Suspension of critical faculties accompanied by literal acceptance of highly suggestive word imagery and sensations is an indicator of entrancing, altered states. When bin Laden and others label those in the West as the infidels, they trigger regressive, literal altered states where blind, uncritical acceptance can occur. The very word "infidel" means unfaithful. Intense focusing and attending creates selective tunnel vision in which regressive, literal states of suggestive acceptance are now possible. The vague reference to God and to how Westerners somehow are inherently unfaithful, betraying God, and are evil and therefore deserve whatever cruelty they get is the great hoax of entrancement. It, in effect, intensely directs Arab and Persian attention and consciousness to a simpleminded, absolutist duality—"if you are not like us and thus like our God/Allah in every and all ways, then you are not one with us or our God/Allah (the One True God) and therefore are the Evil One—The Infidel."

When the terrorists render their politics, cruelty, and subversive activities as cloaked and embedded in the entrancing word and imagery of Allah, their influence is astonishingly pervasive. The entrancing formulation that they are warriors of Allah makes for powerful imagery and uncritical acceptance. This can unleash powerful regression experiences in which childhood trauma, abuse, and other forms of personal violation can be acted out and perpetrated under the name of all that is pious and noble. This is, of course, not a new observation. How many acts of cruelty and savagery have been committed in the name of God or Allah?

To reawaken from such entrancements, the primary association needs to be broken. In the case of the terrorists, when the warrior of Allah has been defeated it becomes clear (though not all at once) that perhaps that warrior may not have been fighting in the name of Allah, but rather in the name of cruelty, selfish narcissism, and psychopathic tendencies.

Yet, entrancement is a powerful altered state and individuals and cultures that are limited, regressive in levels of development, and childlike in their levels of social sophistication will continue to be vulnerable. We all want to believe in ideals and we all have our fantasies and passions. Let us not forget that the suffering and crucifixion of Jesus Christ was no fantasy ideal but a realization of the real-world pain, suffering, and sacrifice involved in creating a more meaningful life in this world—before we go to the next. Arab and Persian terrorists need to reject entrancement and enrich their lives, add diversity, and adopt pluralistic ways of thinking and behaving.

The universe is evolutionary. Life builds upon itself in levels of ever-greater complexity and differentiation. If the unfolding universe is any guide, it would appear that we need to fully enrich with meaning, value, and spirituality the life we are currently in at the level we currently are before we can hope to deserve to move onto a richer, fuller next level or dimension of existence. One life at a time, one level at a time. Maybe if the Arab and Persian cultures are nurtured, encouraged, and enriched to evolve in their own unique formative ways, there will be fewer who are eager to leave them. They need to see the world before they leave it, and that means seeing hope and meaningfulness in their future in this world. There is research to demonstrate that democratic and pluralistic cultures are much less prone to engage in physical conflict and war. Perhaps a chess game (or whatever its equivalent in Arab and Persian cultures) would be a healthier alternative to work out our conflicts than the massive destruction of societies. The time has come for regressive entrancements such as "my God can beat up your God" to be removed so that the maiming and killing of innocent human beings (whether they are different from us or not) stops. Actually, this sounds like it could be the name of a new video game. It certainly would be a welcome relief and a more spiritual elevation toward the next life—in this life.

Chapter 5

SELF-ANNIHILATION AND PYRRHIC VICTORIES

The elimination of terrorism requires that one grasp how terrorism views and constructs its own reality, its own worldview. Terrorism can actually occur in two forms (Elliot, 2002). One form is known as political, with terrorists possessing well-defined goals that may resonate with a more conventional political party. Political terrorism involves violence that does not discriminate between that country's military and civilian population. Examples of this form are the Irish Republican Army and the Stern Gang of Israel. The second form of terrorism is known as millenarian. This form lacks any clear political outcome as well as alignment with any distinct country. The Islamic terrorist groups Al Qaeda (headed by Osama bin Laden), Hamas, and Islamic Jihad (Palestinian terrorist groups) are examples of the second form.

Rohan Gunaratna of the Centre for the Study of Terrorism and Political Violence at the University of St. Andrew's in Scotland conducted an authoritative study of the Al Qaeda terrorist group (Elliot, 2002). He concluded that there is no clear-cut political agenda for the Al Qaeda terrorists in the commonsense understanding of political reality. He goes on to conclude that, rather than a clear objective, the outcome of Al Qaeda is the establishment of a global Islamic caliphate. Bin Laden is described as someone who never interpreted Islam to assist a given political goal. Rather, he notes Islam is his political goal.

Contrasting these forms of terrorism, one can note that political terrorism is more closely aligned with a country and its particular political ideals. It can be reabsorbed—given time and opportunity—back into the mainstream politics of its country. It is amenable to peacekeeping measures (Elliot, 2002). Such were the cases in both South Africa and Ireland.

Millenarian terrorists such as Al Qaeda are not amenable to peace talks, as it where (Elliot, 2002). They are not anchored or associated as a derivative of a country or a culture as are political terrorists. They have been transmuted into an aberrant mutation far beyond affiliation with any country's politics. Transmutations such as these have lost the cultural context of their formative motifs. Such mutations represent a self-serving, cancerous culture. The irony of Islamic jihad is that their fanaticism to extend Islam as a religious end has been at the cost of its cultural roots of motif. It has lost its spiritual motif to incarnate itself onto this earthy plane because of its self-serving nature, not to exist, but to annihilate. This annihilation is not only of the West, but also of itself. Given time and left to its own devices, it might shrivel up, fade away, and ultimately die out. It lost its formative motifs, its cultural contexts in which to grow. Paradoxically, it needs infidels to feed its nihilistic purpose of having a reason to be— which is to destroy what is.

Yet, Al Qaeda continues to thrive with over six thousand members worldwide in small, self-contained cells, or groups. What keeps these cancerous growths from self-extinguishing? They must be fed and supplied (like cancer cells drawing nutrients from the circulation of blood in its host) by partisan sects throughout the world. The Federal Bureau of Investigation and the Central Intelligence Agency have discovered numerous so-called charitable organizations that are really fronts for raising vast sums of money for Al Qaeda. In addition, families of great wealth in Saudi Arabia as well as other countries contribute to Al Qaeda's coffers.

This form of terrorism is fed by those who believe that Islamic fundamentalism is the end in itself. Yet, there is no formative motif expressly designed or manifested on this earthly plane to grow and evolve. There are only rigid, reified fixations imprisoning those subjected to such fundamentalism. This includes rigid ways of dressing women, educating children, and deconstructing men as suicide bombers.

Millenarian terrorists such as Al Qaeda cannot be reabsorbed when they have mutated into a cultural, deconstructive design form that is self-annihilating. Their only purpose is to destroy the others by destroying themselves in the process.

The conflict between India and Pakistan over the Kashmir region threatens to break open another version of such mutations. India has 130 million

Muslims as a minority. If India appears to be anti-Islamic in its conflict with Pakistan over the Kashmir region, it would provide millenarian terrorists more fuel to cite this as another example of Islam itself being attacked.

To understand how mutating forms of terrorism can transmit or radically mutate from a cultural motif, it is critical to contrast Western and Eastern orientations regarding God, religion, and the scientific revolution. As depicted in chapter 3, the universe according to Islam is perfect and unchanging because Allah is the creator of all things who is perfect, ever present, and never changes. Western Christianity also perceives the universe as created by an omnipresent God. Yet, the West sees the universe as unfolding, progressing, and linear in terms of cause and effect. The implications of such a view, which emerged at its zenith in the sixteenth century (the beginning of the scientific revolution) suggests that what God created could be studied, measured, and—to the blasphemy of the Islamic religion—changed by humankind. The magnitude of such a dichotomous construction of metaphysical and universal physical reality has such far-reaching implications in East-West civilizations that the schism has lasted for centuries. The severity of such contrasting operational definitions of each civilization's deity contributes to the mutual perception of the other as infidels and foreign invaders who need containment, if not ultimate extermination (consider the Crusades of the thirteenth century and the Islamic jihad in modern times).

The Islamic religion invokes a sense of enchantment as religion is their way of life in a very literal way (e.g., dress, family roles, work, and rites of passage). In the Catholic Church, for example, priests and nuns wear formal habits of dress. However, Catholic parishioners do not do so when attending church services. Islamic women (the equivalent of parishioners) are expected to wear certain forms of dress as part of their daily activities. The ritualistic observation of the Islamic religion extends far beyond any set place of worship. Their "church" is all of the world (or universe, as the case may be). Enchantment is an essential quality of Islam. It is the ever-present mystery, wonder, and merger of Allah, the universe, and its people in a wondrous splendor of perfect harmony. Such an enchanting splendor is not to be studied, objectified, or improved upon.

Imagine, then, the implications and impact on the Islamic culture when it experiences the West using the scientific method, which separates the participant from the observer. The world and its events can now be studied, analyzed, and evaluated by an observing scientist detached (supposedly anyway) from the experiment he or she is conducting. Improving, changing, and increasing productivity become characteristics of Western civilization, which violate the sense of perfect harmony and stasis of Islamic enchantment.

Ironically, much of the existential crisis of meaningless and purposeless has been attributed to the separation of the person's self from his or her experiences. The extreme isolation of Western men and women from feeling a sense of connection and belonging to the world emerges from this severity of separation of the self from the human and nonhuman world. One doesn't have to be Islamic to discern the sense of personal isolation and loneliness that can exist in modern, industrialized nations. When the scientific revolution occurred in the sixteenth century, a dialectical tension was created between philosophy and God in the Western world. Science eventually took God out of the equation of what reality was (Bloom, 1995).

While the Islamic culture completely immersed itself in the mysterious enchantment of Allah, the universe, and its followers in a stasis of perfect harmony (which limited challenge, change, and experimentation of new ways of being), the West went to the other extreme. The mind and body of the Western person was expunged from the phenomenal world. Instead of feeling a part of and connected to nature, the world, and one another, feeling fully alive, Western men and women became observers, not participants, in their own culture. People became commodities and objects to one another to manipulate and be manipulated, bartering and trading for profit and gain. There was an increasing separation between collecting facts about products and services separate and distinct from intrinsic value.

The intrinsic joy of relating to rocks, trees, one another and so forth was increasingly replaced with objectifications of what could be done with it, to it, and by it. In other words, through the centuries, Western civilization became increasingly focused on how people, places, things, and nature could be of service. God became increasingly separate from the literal rituals of day-to-day functions. The West was capable of symbolizing God in various expressions and transformations suggesting that there were many ways of worshiping. Yet, this has been perceived as the slow erosion of formal religion into secularism, the dilution of God into philosophical questioning, and the loss of mystery, enchantment, and worst of all, faith.

The alienation and depression (as evidenced by increases in teen suicides, job malaise, substance abuse, and violence) demonstrate the harmful effects of objectification on individuals in an increasingly technocratic culture. The onset of modernity and its technology have both increased the quality of products while threatening the sense of personal value. Technology and modernity create wonderful ways of communicating; yet the progressive separation of face-to-face contact of a personal experience becomes less and less frequent. Technology in such a modern culture is now on the verge of artificial intelligence and nanorobotics. Pretty soon we won't need real pets, we can simply program our mechanical dog.

The loss of our ability to be ourselves, to have to play false roles—to make nice when that's not who we really are—has spread to all the modern industrial nations. Poland, France, West Germany, Russia, as well as the United States have all experienced increased rates of suicides (Berman, 1981). The quality of our televisions has vastly increased and the price has gone down. (By the way, so has the handmade craftsmanship that used to make furniture a work of art.) However, the human mind that watches it has somehow been taken over by its programming.

This is not to suggest that progress, growth, and development are not good, only that it, like Islamic enchantment, they can have devastating extremes.

THE 10TH PLANET—U.S.A.

America is the survivor of the cold war and, thus, the only superpower in the world. Many dictatorships have fallen throughout the world giving rise to democratic regimes. The United States far surpasses any other country in its cultural expansion of motifs involving the silicon revolution, advanced technology, and information processing (DeSousa, 2002). American culture in the form of music, movies, ideas, and modernity are deeply influential throughout the world.

The deconstruction of the Soviet Union and other dictatorial regimes has given rise to a more pluralistic world of competing factions and warring conflicts (such as in Kosovo and Chechnya). The world has become a more dangerous place (DeSousa, 2002) and is resistant to globalization that appears to replace totalitarian governments with an all-encompassing uniformity of Western culture (read as Americanization) as the ruling culture of the world.

Huntington (DeSousa, 2002) expressed that post–cold war conflicts could merge all the "fault lines" between the world's civilizations. Such a reference is actually to the world's major religions (Islam, Christianity, Confucianism, Hinduism, etc.). The proliferation of Western civilization throughout the world with emerging democracies in Latin America, Eastern Europe and so forth translates into a Judeo-Christian orientation.

When a country's expansionism translates into one of an entire civilization with emerging religious roots, cultural clash of motifs is inevitable. These cultural motifs of multiple civilizations collide into one another, threatening conflicts, like tectonic plates creating enormous pressures erupting into world.

The collision of Western and Eastern civilizations ultimately emerges as one of colliding religions. Religious wars are deadly (read nihilistic), as one is not only fighting for one's country and way of life, but also for his or her god—the ultimate value of life after life.

Unfortunately, being the world's only superpower has set up America as the target. America has become the giant to be assaulted by the Davids of the world. Such a perceived role for America can be quite dangerous. Anti-American sentiment can run deep, but hidden, in the false smiles of other countries that enjoy our prosperity but resent our cultural intrusion. Even our allies in Europe (e.g., France) see the United States as arrogant, which is unjustified in their eyes. It is the McWorld domination that may help their economies, but erode their cultural motifs.

This collision course of civilizations is accelerated by American-style globalization that is capable of reaching cataclysmic, epic proportions as West meets East. The East (Islamic religious leaders) perceive problems of how to selectively import Western technology and prosperity while filtering through existential crises, dehumanization, and other unwanted value corruptions connected to a postmodern culture. The Islamic East is a blatant example of civilizations seeking to reap the benefits of the West's (read American) abundance, yet preserving their own culture.

The Islamic East, because of its culturally unique motif of operationalizing (a behavioral description of a construct) Allah in reified ways, is blinded to how the West articulates its own spirituality in such highly individualized motifs. It cannot understand how eclecticism and secularism could have any spirituality in God. While there may well be an emphasis on materialism and at times corporate greed, it is intriguing that research (Kelley, 2002) into what motivates American workers reveals that money ranks fourth. Recognition, meaningful contributions, and making a genuine difference all command higher priorities. American motifs (e.g., cowboys, farmers, and heroic entrepreneurs) reflect expressions of a young culture. The almost obsessive emphasis on youthfulness in America parallels the cultural reality that America is, by world standards, a young country growing out of colonial origins. There is a brashness and, at times, a cultural tendency to "be real," be unpretentious, and avoid being one of the "foo foo" people, as one American waitress expressed to me, in November 2002, while working in an American bistro.

By contrast, American mothers who work, leaving their children with baby-sitters, and unfaithful fathers, who practice indiscriminant sexual activity and promiscuity, typify how Americans are perceived by the East. While there are definitely many deficits in any culture, the East character-izes Western civilization and American motifs in such stereotyped schemes.

The East wants no part of these schematic motifs. Islamic critics argue that there is no selectivity possible. Their critique is that modernity is actu-ally Western civilization's motif in itself. To them, the very concept of America is a subversive ideal (DeSousa, 2002). If such a concept is allowed into the East, it will produce an enormous social upheaval that will eliminate a religious basis for their society. It is interesting to note that in the 1950s, many older Americans viewed Elvis ("the Pelvis") Presley also as subversive in his corruption of America's youth with the most deadly of evils, rock and roll. The same view was held in 1939 by Nazi Germany regarding what was then known as another radical aberration of music and moral corruption—swing! Can you believe Adolph Hitler wor-ried that swing kids, as they were known then, would corrupt the integrity of his Nazi Germany?

The Islamic East fears a displacement of its own cherished motifs of value. They worry that the formative design of their civilization will be unrecognizable. This is where the terrorists chime in, vis-à-vis bin Laden, that "Islam is facing the greatest threat to its survival since the days of Mohammed" (DeSousa, 2002). Unfortunately, to the Islamic fundamen-talists, change, evolution, and derivations of their traditional motifs into more sophisticated formativeness are indeed seen as a threat. Instead of growing archaic and traditional Islamic motifs into their own advanced evolutionary forms, they hold on to the reified past for dear life—or death as the case may be. Yet, this is precisely what one would expect from a cul-tural motif based on an operational definition of Allah as unchanging, per-fect, and a mystery incapable of being fathomed by humans—to even the most marginal of degrees.

Yet, prior to the sixteenth century, Islamic civilization was highly pros-perous and rich in social advances. It certainly found ways of reconc-iling social prosperity and raised the standard of living with a perfect, unchangeable, nonevolutionary universe directed by Allah, in which man never attempted to understand it. Ironically, the astronomical theories and writings of Ptolemy, as well as Chinese scientists of the time, were translated into Arabic and critiqued as to how they could be more accurate in their depiction of the solar system. Apparently, it is permissible for Islamic scientists (an oxymoron according to their religion) to exert attempts at understanding the universe, as long as it is restricted to a select few and not a cultural way of life. Plato, when he wrote the *Republic,* challenged such cultural motifs when he espoused leading "the examined life." As a consequence, the Greeks were also seen as a threat and were challenged.

The more contemporary view of cultural motifs in collision is how Islam views American television. It is seen as disgusting, as is the way they perceive our youth as corrupted. The West, as represented to Islam by America, has lost its spirituality, become atheistic, and is like a viral disease that is spreading throughout the world.

The Islamic critic, Sayyid Qutb, expressed his fear that the West is engaging in spiritual colonialism. The only deterrent is to destroy the influence of the West from within its own cultural motif (DeSousa, 2002). The extent that such views become radicalized raises the specter that either the East breaks the West's will to evolve itself or the West culturally annihilates the East by its very existence. Such paradoxical loops are perpetuated by permeable, even porous, cultural boundaries.

The hypersensitivity of one culture to another that lets itself become infected, as it were, (rather than culturally enriched) by another's cultural mores demonstrates its own vulnerability. Rather than the East (read Islamic culture) mature, evolve, and enrich its own cultural sophistication (How can it do that if it doesn't believe in the evolution of its own species?), it solves its vulnerability by annihilating the other (read America).

Actually, the Islamic culture between 1200 and 1400 was quite advanced and evolved compared with other cultures (e.g., in science, architecture, and education). After colonialism by the West of the East ensued in the last 500 years, periods of decline began to set in. Yet, even in the enlightened period of Islamic culture, there was still a powerful merger between religion and state (or way of life). God (or Allah) was never separated from society or government, as it has been in the West. Such a separation is literally foreign to the East and in itself a sign of religious infidelity. Similar perceptions of the West occur regarding constructs of evolutionary time and development, as how can man ever hope to improve the perfection of

Allah's universe? Intriguingly, it was in the ninth to thirteenth centuries where Christianity shifted its time constructs of a spiraling, repetitious universe toward one of linear and developmental cause and effect. It was this shift that reoriented Western Christianity toward discovery and eventual emergence out of the dark ages.

The Islamic submission to Allah (especially in its most literal form of fundamentalism) far surpasses a mere set of beliefs. Such submission is a complete absorption of self into religious experience. While Western Christianity conveys man as surrendering to God, the methodology of each person finding his or her own path (as in the saying "all roads lead to Rome") is highly prized in Western society as freedom to choose and how to be. Such liberalism is viewed as bordering on secularism by the East and held in great disdain. The West is perceived as obsessed with freedom for its own sake—almost as a God in itself.

GLARING DIFFERENCES

With such stark and dramatic differences between cultures, cohabitation in a global economy becomes more and more stressful. America and the rest of the West may need to realize that the democratic qualities of freedom, independence, and cookie-cutter diversity (each culture is supposed to fit neatly into others) actually are toxic to other cultures of the East. To the East, American democratic values (which we idealize and for which we would give our lives) is a toxic poison to traditional Islamic religious experiences. There is an old adage that "one man's meat is another man's poison." If the West is perceived as trying to force-feed the world with Big Macs (as in the McWorld phenomenon) (Hassner, 2002), other cultures such as those in the East can experience that we are trying to poison their way of life.

DIET OF GLOBALIZATION

Terrorism prospers in such a contextual set of political and global conditions. The cultural clash perceived as creating toxic, poisonous conditions for one another's culture can lead to survivalist thinking and behaving. Columnist Barbara Ehrenreich (DeSousa, 2002) has written that the United States is responsible for vast global inequities in which terrorism is rooted. These sentiments were applauded by black caucuses that said America must stop and that the world is not for sale.

Terrorists groups, such as Al Qaeda and Hamas, feed off the toxins and poisons of dissent, inequity, and fear mongering. Without demonstrating contextual respect for each culture's unique motif and idiosyncratic manifestations, globalization will only feed the toxic hunger of world terrorism.

Self-annihilation becomes the existential (or nonexistential) purpose for being among terrorist groups. It can always justify its venomous ways by projecting blame for their rage on some infidel threatening the Islamic culture's extinction. America and the West feed right into their hands by refusing to develop cultural sensitivity to the unique, intricate motifs that all cultures convey. This occurs through the rapid, corporate expansion of Western industrialized nations presenting itself as globalization. As will be presented later, such an expansion presents coercive and dangerous repercussions for the United States and the West in general. The threats from militant Islamic groups such as the Taliban, Hamas, and Al Qaeda emerge because of radicalization of extreme sects in the East. Poverty and low quality of life are not necessarily causal factors. This was addressed in earlier chapters. The leader of the highjackers of the September 11 horror, Mohammed Atta, was well educated and enjoyed a relatively satisfying level of economic functioning. His alienation from achieving higher-level goals in his country (e.g., not being admitted to graduate university and stymied in his career) was an aggravating factor that contributed to his sense of alienation and eventual turn to terrorism. It was a twisted turn in that, rather than dealing with the origin of his domestic frustration, he turned on the West, projecting and blaming the United States for his lifestyle limitations.

The dynamics of aspiring and striving for higher levels of achievement and life quality are not new to countries transitioning into postmodernity. The peoples of Saudi Arabia, Pakistan, Iran and so forth are increasingly exposed to higher standards of living. When they see the quality of life in the West, with its advanced technology and cultural forms of entertainment, they are accelerated into a catch-up modality of wanting it all now. While the West has been developing and innovating for decades, the East has remained, essentially, status quo.

Globalization, especially of a corporate nature, has thrust goods and services into the East's culture, which has not nurtured and nor designed internal structures supporting growth and advancement of the culture from within. For example, the advent of introducing cell phones and Internet services into the East may provide sophistication of communication services. It does not sophisticate what and how individuals, such as

Mohammed Atta, learn how to communicate their individual needs in civilized, assertive ways. It is like dangling carrots on a stick without providing an infrastructure on how to reach them.

This phenomenon of higher-level striving leading to violence and destruction is not new. In the 1960s and 1970s, prominent American universities such as Harvard and the University of California—Los Angeles experienced student protests, not only against the war in Vietnam, but against the "repressive" system of the military-industrial complex. Students from some of the most liberal universities in the country proclaimed their freedoms were being violated. These students, however, did not fly planes into the university's administration building. There were, however, numerous unpaid pizza bills and long-distance phone charges left.

In some ways, the East is slowly transitioning from a status quo of limited internal lifestyle development into postmodernity. There is shock, realization of limited development, real frustration, and a sense of hopelessness. Such are the cultural breeding grounds of terrorism sprouting like weeds in a barren garden of stymied cultural motifs.

When cell phones were introduced into the Philippines before the people had a chance to adapt to their use, paralysis and intense frustration were inevitable. Waving the postmodern carrot without assisting a culture to develop a step-wide ladder of growing up motifs to reach it increases the probability of more Atta's in the world.

The militant Islamic movement is the East's response to its twisted perception that the West is the cause of its cultural impoverishment to deal with an increasing globalized world connectedness. Perceiving the West's advances throughout Europe and the Mideast (Israel) and its troops stationed strategically in the Mediterranean, militant Islamics are convinced that the West wants to dominate their culture. As a consequence, they may have experiences similar to countries having faced the threat of fascism and communism (Pipes, 2002). Theirs is a deeply "bruised sense of identity" (Pipes, 2002).

It is at this level of hierarchy of needs (Maslow, 1968) that need frustration and hopelessness make them most dangerous and violent. All life-forms seek to perpetuate themselves, and the Islamic culture is no different. Currently, it appears that the Islamic desire is to propagate itself, which includes "conquering America" (Pipes, 2002). This may come in the form of violence or in the form of conversion. Currently, the Muslim American culture is one of the fastest growing (read conversion rate) in the United States.

AMERICAN TALIBAN

There are examples of this conversion process in the American caught fighting for the Taliban in Afghanistan. Allegedly, John Walker Lindh had come from what may be termed a good home in America and converted to Islam. H. Rap Brown is another example of such a process. In the 1930s, Elijah Muhammad became head of the Nation of Islam (Pipes, 2002). After 40 years its radical perspectives have now been habituated and accepted as mainstream among the Muslim community in America. There are many concerns about the American Muslims and the potential conflict with American Jews.

There are, however, varied Islamic groups less militant than others. The republic of Turkey seems to typify such deviations of moderate Islamic Muslims. It is quite difficult to reconcile varying factions. When prominent Islamics, such as the Lebanese writer Samihatef El-Zein, proclaims that Islamic law accounts for all events and all problems through its explanations (Pipes, 2002), closed-minded grandiosity are the consequences. This is the problem of fundamentalist extremes that merge, literally, the spiritual letter of the law with the specificities of economics, education, and cultural development.

Yet, if one looks to the West, fundamentalist trends can be found in the extreme conservative right of Christians in America. They, too, believe their Christian law explains and accounts for all problems and events. Case in point is their absolutist view on prolife in all cases at all times. Even if they have to murder doctors to do it, they are going to "save life at any cost." Such conservative, Christian extremists advocate the death penalty while professing that DNA testing, which has freed hundreds of prisoners from death row, is a mere technicality. Their view is "right is right," no matter what.

As will be seen in future chapters, such fundamentalist extremes endanger the existence of the general cultural motif, but initially serve the purpose of asymmetrically counterbalancing trends that appear at first to destabilize that motif. This is known as backlash and represents a culture's way of seeking balance through asymmetry. That is, extremes at one level (e.g., radical liberalism and loss of guidelines) create higher-level conservative extremes in government and religious mergers.

Note that Islamic fundamentalism has merged religion with government, lifestyle, and education. Ironically, there is a strong merger between such conservatives in America (e.g., Jerry Falwell), who many believe have the ear of our president, George W. Bush. After all, it was the conservative right that was of such critical assistance in the primaries that ultimately propelled Mr. Bush into the presidency.

As of this writing, President Bush has advocated going to war with Iraq as the only way to protect America after the horror of 9/11. Yet, for the last 10 years, America preferred to keep Saddam Hussein in power to prevent the Shiite Islamic sect from taking power. Fundamentalism in any form has a life of its own, violent and dynamic. These dynamics, while seeking to propagate one's cultural motifs, threaten to constrict and choke off its formative lifeblood. One of the greatest risks to going to war with Iraq is to inflame the entire Islamic region. They already believe America and the rest of the West want to recolonialize them (as they did in the middle centuries). If America unilaterally attacks Iraq without demonstrating the immediate, imminent danger, this would only confirm the Islamic world's worst case scenario that the West will not stop until the Islamic culture is eliminated.

The next chapter engages the need for cultures to initiate a dialectical exchange and interfacing of their unique cultural motifs to reset boundaries and initiate genuine global synergy.

Chapter 6

EVOLUTION OF INFIDELS INTO MULTIFACETED MOTIFS

To say that Eastern and Western cultures misunderstand one another is the understatement of the millennium. While Christianity and Islam are monotheistic, these religions (and the ways in which they are acculturated) are quite distinct from one another. The cultural mores, ways of worship, and degrees of cultural-social fusion are all variant from one another.

Understanding that we really don't understand one another is the first step toward making space and time for a dialectical interaction between unique cultural motifs. There is a real danger in comparing religions and the cultures they infuse, as the variations and deviations can be numerous and diverse. This, in itself, makes comparing Christianity and Islam a precarious exercise, for what does one really mean when generalizations for religions are used? Before launching into religious variations and derivations, it is important to highlight a central theme, which is that each cultural motif is a unique, idiosyncratic entity, or life-form, of that civilization. It embodies the lifeblood of that culture's core characteristics and even personality. To speak of an American motif is to capture that unique characterization of integrated core qualities. These can include fierce independence, candor, rugged individualism, humor, the pursuit of the American dream, and in times of crisis—emergence of heroic patriotism.

It is the particular flavor and degree of integration of these core characteristics that articulates American motifs. For example, the concept of being a down-to-earth person, not obsessed with formality and pomp and circumstance, adds a flavor of being a "real person" in the American motif.

One waitress in a Chicago bistro chagrined when she spoke of the "foo foo" people—the ones who tended to "put on airs."

The curiosity about American motifs is that they are pluralistic in their multiculturalism. This is at the heart of being American, in being one's own unique self. However, there is a paradox here. While the American motif is about being the land of opportunity for diverse cultures from around the world, there are certain pop culture derivatives of the American motif that clearly qualify what is American about its motif.

When Americans see Muslim women dressed in burkhas and other unique cultural clothing, it is clear that this is not the way Americans as a whole dress. Fitting diverse cultures into one American motif of a land of opportunity requires tolerance and mutual adjustment between new and resident citizens. Many people coming to America are amazed at how enormous our country is. This is not so much in terms of geography as in the vast range of choices in material goods. The motif of America involves "bigger is better" and "more for your money" mentalities. The freedom of choice, characteristic of America's motif, is daunting to many who arrive here from foreign countries.

Yet, with enormous freedoms come personal responsibility and self-mastery. If one is not raised and acculturated to the theory and practice of responsible choices in personal freedom, one can be overwhelmed and culture shock can set in. America's motif of informality allows for rich mosaics of individual and cultural diversity. This all hinges on individuals' ability to master responsibly their freedoms. Because of a motif built on the premise of "the land of the free and the home of the brave," there is no formal structure or design that guides or directs people to what they should do or how they should live.

POP CULTURE AS PARENT

The emergence in America of what is known as pop culture involves a motif within a motif of what is American. The wide range of music styles (rap, hip-hop, country, jazz, rock and roll) as well as Hollywood movies, fashion, and styles, exert powerful influences and messages onto the masses as to what's "in," "cool," and acceptable (and what is not). The enriching qualities of all this offer a plethora of wonderful choices of what each person may freely want to pursue. The dark side of pop culture's influence is the enormous pressure to conform to ways of acting, being, dressing, and talking (or how someone supposedly is not in, acceptable, or significant). Extreme versions of these pressures to conform can be seen in the tragedy of violence in our high schools where in Littleton, Colorado, two teenagers who were bullied and harassed for not being "with it" in Columbine High School's pop culture went on a shooting rampage, killing or wounding dozens of students before they themselves were killed.

There is enormous, informal pressure in the pop culture motif of America to act and be a certain way. Because of the vast ranges of freedom of choice in America, even Americans born and raised here can, at times, be overwhelmed. Young boys without fathers are extremely vulnerable because America does not provide a clear social-cultural structure to assist young people to mature and self-manage. Freedom has its blessings, but it also has its curses. While our schools and sporting institutions are supposed to provide design and structure, it is all too easy for individuals to fall between the cracks and get lost in such systems. Beneath the façade of informality and down-to-earth qualities of the American motif lie a highly complex network of institutional settings. From the family system of birth, its extensions of uncles, grandparents, and so on, to neighborhood communities and clichés, educational systems, and various clubs to business organizations, recreational theme parks, malls, coffee shops, legal systems, gender roles, and age levels—the web of interconnecting social-cultural domains is vast and intricate.

Throughout all of this permeates the motif of pop culture as an operating, behavioral expression of the American motif. If you look out on any street in America, you will see a vast majority of people dressed in informal casual wear. They speak casually, may act casually, and even think casually in conversation. Yet, beneath this layer lies the enormous, complex labyrinth of institutional webs structured under the illusion of freedom without pressure.

Many people came to America believing all the pop culture exported as the land of milk and honey (commonly known as Hollywood). The world perceives America's motif through its music, cinemas, and fashion of a pop culture's motif that emerges from a Hollywood prototype. When they get here, they are shocked to discover that everyone doesn't have the Hollywood glamour or riches. In fact, they discover the highly casual "formal wear" of T-shirts, jeans, baseball caps, and gym shoes (that cost a fortune, by the way). The Americanization of Muslims into mainstream pop culture can be quite stressful for an Islamic culture that has more formal, above-board structure and design. This is partially because of the stronger fusion of Islamic religion with the social practices of their culture. Pop culture to the Islamic civilization is foreign to them. The Islamic attire is more formally aligned with religious as well as social-cultural principles.

Ironically, the informality of Western pop culture has a kind of uniformity of its own. That is, variant derivatives of pop culture's casual attire, including decorated T-shirts, jeans and baggy pants, and gym shoes (in their emboldened sizes and designs), stem from their core motif schematic of T-shirt, jeans, and gym shoes (with a possible baseball cap thrown in for good measure). While reflecting a powerful differentiation from religion and state, peer and socialization pressures of approval seeking, fitting in, and seeking significance of belonging (social identity) all exert powerful conformity influences. There was a cartoon depicted in the 1960s of a group of protesting hippies all wearing long hair, blue jeans, sandals, and beards, carrying signs that read nonconformists. There can be a powerful "tyranny of the majority," as Alexis de Tocqueville had described about America, in its influences on the individual. Noam Chomsky (2001) has described America (and its motif) as "one of the most fundamentalist countries in the world." While this is not necessarily a bad thing, it does lend itself to the highly structured, complex design of America's pop culture motif.

The appearance of everyone able to do their own thing as long as it is not illegal or harmful to self or others creates an illusion of permissiveness and open-endedness that is deceiving. The constitution of the United States guarantees inalienable rights to every citizen of America. However, to be granted acceptance, approval, and significance in our social-cultural motif, powerful influences previously described are at work that affect the quality of our lives. Alfred Adler (Ansbacher & Ansbacher, 1956), one of Freud's students, described how critical it is for human beings to experience a sense of belonging. This sense of belonging affects the individual's self-esteem, life purpose, and degree of social identity. Each individual has free will and freedom of choice. Yet, these innate abilities and attributes do not occur in a vacuum. They affect and are affected by the context of the particular cultural motif with which they interact. America has become a highly complex society with multicultural influences seeking common denominators to which we can all connect.

MODERNITY IN AMERICA

There is nothing free about freedom in America. Thriving and arriving in a successful lifestyle involving family, career, relationships, personal fulfillment, and financial and spiritual unfolding requires hard work and mastery. Years of acculturation, education, and socialization are required for one to learn to exercise good judgment, healthy choices, and to select meaningful goals. Having some fun wouldn't be so bad either if we could squeeze that into our incredulous, multitask lifestyles (ongoing learning, running a family, dual career marriages, etc.). How about just being able to pay all those credit card bills, get the new DVDs and the latest car models out of Detroit, and take your family to Disney World? Affording all the goodies of materialism is expensive.

As of this printing, America is experiencing a rising unemployment rate of 6 percent (*New York Times,* 2002), an increasing financial difference between those with wealth and those less fortunate, and growing anger and anxiety over future job security. There is growing sentiment for joining unions and protesting corporate corruption in America (vis-à-vis the financial scandals at Enron, Arthur Anderson, WorldCom, etc.). Even in the land of the free and the home of the brave, politics, power, and positioning in the culture exerts enormous influence upon the quality of the individual's lifestyle.

The postmodern information age, acceleration in advanced technology, and virtual reality dimensions (movies with virtual actors, virtual astronauts, virtual war games, and virtual partners) are additional influences affecting quality of life. While we have more gadgets and conveniences (and yes, tremendous advancements in science, the Human Genome Project, and the expanding universe of the Hubble telescope), we also experience less human personal contact.

Wholey (1988) once said that the average human being requires 25 hugs a day. He didn't mean the kind you get while being arrested. The potential for loneliness, depression, alcoholism and substance abuse, and perverse crimes (such as those committed against women and children) has not been abated in our depersonalized, postmodern culture.

TIP OF THE CULTURAL MOTIF

The aforementioned are but a few of the social-cultural dynamics and influences affecting and being affected by the American motif and that of its pop culture. The rest of the world, vis-à-vis the East, only comprehends the tip of the vast complexity of what it means to be an American and the evolutionary (if not, at times, revolutionary) changes that are transpiring in our country. To further add to the complexity, which Americans are we talking about? There are many. There is the American motif as exemplified by those living in the great southwest (e.g., the Texas mentality). There is the eastern seaboard with its liberal intelligence. There is the heartland of America (e.g., Chicago—the city that works—and it does quite obsessively). Then of course there is the west coast (e.g., California with its magnificent beauty, color, and Hollywood mystique). The French tend to gravitate to California as it matches part of their motif of artistic color and iridescent brilliance of light. California is the only place I've ever been where they applaud the beauty of its sunsets (e.g., Big Sur).

While we are all Americans, our ways of exemplifying and manifesting our freedoms and lifestyles can boggle the imagination. During the cold war, it was once said that if the Russians ever tried to invade from the west coast, they would never make it past Las Vegas for wanting to open up their own franchises (e.g., casinos and McDonald's). Does this mean that their culture's motifs would have been compromised? Perhaps they would have to some extent. Yet, the fierce competition and striving for superiority would illustrate qualities that paralleled the former Soviet Union and the United States.

RIGID CONSTRUCTS, FLEXIBLE DEVIATIONS

Communism and capitalism in theory are diametrically opposed to one another. Yet, applications of derivative forms can create surprising collaborations. While this is the art of politics and statesmanship, it is also the realm of formative motifs and the evolution of derivative formativeness. Proliferating capitalism and communism created a tremendous struggle for survival. The Cuban missile crisis, the race for space and the moon, nuclear superiority, the Berlin wall—all evidenced a dualistic battle fiercely competing for superiority.

The end of the cold war occurred with the star wars program of President Ronald Reagan. The vast financial expenditures of the Soviet Union trying to keep up with the United States eventually crushed it into financial ruin. However, the Soviet Union, in seeking to keep pace and outstrip America, had evolved more and more derivational forms of functioning like the United States and vice versa. These countries with their opposite ideologies had evolved derivational motifs in ways of operating of increasing similarity. For example, the Soviet Union's original motif of working together collectively as a group, de-emphasizing individual merits, began to change. Their cosmonauts became highly and individually revered. Soviet scientists began to take individual pride in their accomplishments in superior rocket thrust engines that they developed. The competition with the United States stimulated a level of functioning that required the Soviets to become progressively "capitalistic" in behavioral functioning in order to keep up with the United States. It forced a formative shift in derivational motives that eventually undermined the very ideology of communism. The art of war might suggest that the first step toward evolutionary change is to engage the opponent who has opposing ideological motifs in an equal and escalating exchange until the differences between the two begin to blur. The motif, which is most compatible with those formative motif derivatives, will be most likely to stay the course.

EAST MEETS WEST

The September 11 attacks on America were very different from the long-term escalation of the cold war. Back in the days when the Soviet Union invaded Afghanistan, the United States funded terrorist groups with leaders, such as bin Laden, to resist the communist invaders. Yet, these very terrorists whose motifs the United States supported turned on America. Events such as Somalia where United States Marines were attacked, the existence of military bases from the Gulf War that terrorists like bin Laden viewed as violations of Islamic sacred ground, and the assault on the U.S.S. *Cole* in the Mediterranean are all events linked and leading up to the September 11 assault on American territory.

The Islamic motif of fusing religion with politics is markedly different from the ideological conflict of the cold war. The similar forms of competitiveness between the United States and Soviet Union do not exist between the West (America and Europe) and the Islamic East. As has been extensively presented earlier, there is a marked distinction between the American motif of freedom in diversity from that of the Islamic fusion of religion and social-cultural behavior.

The East's construction of motif can appear totalitarian and tyrannical. Yet, this is as misleading as trying to stereotype all of America as the pop culture of Hollywood. The Islamic merging of religion with precise social and cultural behaviors and prescribed rituals is foreign to the West. America and its allies understandably view democracy as the system of government for the whole world. This is their motif, their life-form that seeks propagation and expansion as all life-forms do. The old adage of "if you're not with us, you're against us" is a dangerous and misleading form of dualistic thinking.

ASYMMETRICAL MOTIFS

Motifs by definition are asymmetrical in that they have their own unique, idiosyncratic, multifaceted way of expressing themselves (Feeney, 2001). They are not unlike fractals that are patterns that repeat themselves in self-similar but ever-unique derivational patterns. The Islamic fusion of religion and social-cultural behavior and rituals may seem oppressive and untowardly to the rich diversity of the West, with its separation and freedom of church and state and culture. It is that very asymmetry of comparative motifs that appears oppositional and threatening to both the East and the West.

To the Islamic holy man (as well as to terrorists such as bin Laden), the West's separation of church, state, and secular culture smacks of an un-Godlike way of life. The Islamic culture cannot comprehend how the West can embrace spiritual holiness with such a separation. To them it appears that our pop culture is our God of worship. When the terrorists attacked the World Trade Center, they were attacking the symbol of financial materialism that supports that pop culture and all the un-Godly.

The Muslims who live in America continue to integrate and fuse religion with their social and cultural behavior and mores. They continue to wear the burkha and they are selective as to their music, cinemas, and peer groups with whom they may associate. Yet, they can live and be loyal Americans because they can tolerate the American way of life, that is, to tolerate differences. How can they do this without seeing the rest of America as spirituality bankrupt infidels? It is because they are a moderate derivative of the Islamic motif. Those who come to this country are Muslims who can embrace the spirituality of other Americans without having to fundamentalize their way or ours.

It is important to remember that we are still dealing with asymmetrical motifs. That is, it is not an opposite form of motif but rather the nonmirrored image reverse of our motif. The nonmirrored image reverse is in reference to logic and linguistic reasoning. It means that the relationship of one construct or set of themes to another is not diametrically opposite to or inverted, but rather angular. For example, if one proposes that "all men are mortal," then the opposite would be "all men are immortal." The inverted would be "not all men are mortal." The nonmirrored image reverse would be "not not all men are mortal." The American motif is the nonmirrored image reverse of the Islamic motif in that it is not not a fusion of religious and social-cultural principles, but rather a mosaic of tolerance allowing for both possibilities without insisting on one or the other. This is the manifestation of cultural diversity as sanctioned by our government. Such a diversity, or metalevel (tolerance for intolerance), is not allowed for in the Islamic motif. It is such angular configurations that create asymmetry between cultural motifs. That is why there is such great misunderstanding between our cultural motifs. Nothing is worse than to believe we understand what we really don't understand. That is one of the contributing dynamics that threatens the relationships between Eastern and Western West cultural motifs.

DIALECTICAL TENSION

There needs to be a dialectical exchange comparing and contrasting the asymmetry of our cultural motifs. This would allow for at least an understanding that neither the East nor West are infidels, but are so divergent as to appear un-Godly in form, but not in substance.

As in America with its variance of motif derivations throughout, there is some variance in Islam. There are two branches of Islam, Sunni and Shia (Rammelkamp, 2002). The Sunni Muslim maintains that he is his own priest. Essentially, Sunni Islam believes that the divine relationship between Allah and man is individualistic. Following the right path means that Allah can do whatever He wants with each man. Leadership ability, moral character, and knowledge were the selection criteria for election into power as the caliphate. The Shiites believe that leadership in the Islamic religion is more dependent on divine grace. This meant that lineage as a direct descendant of Muhammad, the Prophet, is the critical determinant for leadership as a Muslim. Their belief is of God having chosen people, in that He is closer to some people (known as imams) than to others. According to Rammelkamp (2002), there have been a total of 11 imams who have lineage connections of heredity to Ali. When Muhammad died, there were no directions left as to how to determine succession. Shortly after his death, important Muslim figures placed the father-in-law of Muhammad, Abu Bakr, as the secular head of Islam. In time, Muhammad's cousin and son-in-law, Ali, was provoked into the caliphate in A.D. 656 but was assassinated after only five years. By then, Ali had settled in central Iraq. The severity of schism between the Sunni and Shiite Muslims has been maintained in modern times, as evidenced by the vicious conflict between Iraq and Iran some years ago.

Such schisms within Islam reflect a rigidity of all-or-nothing categories (e.g., individual relationship with Allah as compared to being one of the chosen). It is representative of the difficulty of relating and integrating divergent motifs to one another.

The difficulty of cultural motifs cohabitating with one another, especially when infused with religious orientations, becomes quite severe. The need for a dialogue and exchange between cultures is well known. Yet, without a genuine dialectical exchange (a meaningful comparing and contrasting of unique, idiosyncratic qualities of the culture's motif itself), only superficial and cookie-cutter accommodations are made. Witness that America, Europe, and the Mideast have rich and extensive integrated societies. Yet, prejudice, racism, and intolerance have not subsided. In Europe, there are actually increased sentiments of anti-Semitism and anti-Americanism. While there are multiple dynamics that contribute toward prejudice, the inability (or unwillingness) to deconstruct stereotypes revealing unique cultural motifs is a major impediment.

As will be presented, divergent cultural motifs actually function in symbiotic (mutually beneficial) ways. When the synergy between unique cultural motifs is articulated in ways that depict their idiosyncratic coming together and moving apart, high levels of coexistence can be demonstrated. The risk in cultural exchanges involves the cookie-cutter approach to multicultural motifs that undermine what makes each uniquely distinct.

America is considered the most culturally diverse country in the world. Yet, there are strong stereotypes and categorical ways of "cookie cutting" various racial and ethnic groups. While they may not necessarily be disrespectful or intolerant, they can reflect oversimplification and ignorance. For example, how many Americans really understand what Islam really is or why the burkha is worn? How does America, which promotes a pop culture advocating *American Idol* television shows emphasizing fame and popularity, really accommodate to strict religious fusion in the Islamic lifestyle?

Contrast our American pop culture with that of the Taliban and Osama bin Laden's severity of rigid, literal thinking. They are Wahhabi Islamics who are followers of their religious leader, al-Wahhab, who lived from 1699 to 1792. Their belief is to follow the letter of Allah's law. There is no room for symbolism and interpretation. Their motif is to strip away any form of ostentation from Islam and restore its purity.

Fundamental Islam has always adhered to strict Wahhabi interpretations of the Koran since its inception (Santos, 2002). This sect is sustained and has its home in Saudi Arabia, but it has spread throughout the Muslim world.

One can realize the difficulty of coexistence with such rigid and literal forms of cultural motifs imbued with such religious orientations. Attempts to create coexistence between and amongst such cultural divergences can lead to an all-or-nothing, win-lose scenario. The Islamic fundamentalists are by definition an extremist form of the religion. Yet, as has been described, there are variant and other divergent forms (e.g., Sunni and Shiite). The Islamic fundamentalist presents an asymmetrical cultural variant as compared to America's pop culture.

This asymmetrical contrast is expressed in a number of dimensions. The pop culture of America is primarily defined within the nation-state status of our country. By contrast, Islamic fundamentalism is nonlocalized pervasively spreading throughout the world and a number of nation-states. While it is true that America exports its culture, its origins and centrality of operation remain in the hands of America.

Another asymmetrical contrast between these cultures is the very nature of their core principles. America is founded on principles designed to enhance the quality of life of the individual while on this Earth. The domain of Islamic fundamentalists (and to a lesser extent the other variant forms of Islam) is not of this Earth. It is in the next life, if you will. This is very different from the struggle America had with the Soviet Union. They were very much on the same playing field of survival on this earthly plane. As a result, conventional deference using a mutually assured destruction (MAD) strategy was effective. That is because there was symmetry at the same level of reality and organization between the cultures. Principles may be diametrically opposed, but the symmetry between cultures in terms of their similarity and balance (e.g., operating at the same level of organization and desiring the same types of outcome) was very high.

Also, the core of America and its pop culture are materialistic in expression (e.g., achieving, acquiring possessions and wealth, raising healthy productive children, etc.). Because the Islamic culture adheres to a literal word of Allah, fuses its religion to its lifestyle, and takes the word of Allah literally (vis-à-vis the written word of the Koran), there is no investment in materialistic outcomes. Their domain is not of this world. Therefore, how does one compete and coexist with (or even defeat) a nonmaterial investment that has no capital, nationhood, or property? Even their education in

Taliban schools in Afghanistan (before the United States removed them) focused on teaching their children not how to live, but how to die (e.g., suicide bombing and jihad).

Asymmetry can also be discerned in the way or processes utilized by these cultures in terms of growth. America and the West focus on the future, growth, and evolution of the possibility of a better tomorrow. The Islamic fundamentalists don't have a future (perhaps in more ways than just one) on this Earth. If we don't destroy them, they may self-destruct on their own (given enough room and latitude to their obsession with violence as a means to the end). They have no concept of evolution in the universe or in their own culture, and theirs is the literal reading of Allah having created a perfect universe and it is human beings who are problematic. Accordingly, it is not the world's problems or the universe that must change or be solved (they are not solution-oriented thinkers in terms of bettering their quality of life, only in destroying that of the infidel other). How does one negotiate or resolve problems into solutions when the existence of a problem with the world is declared nonexistent and that you should be killed for proclaiming that a problem exists. At times, this sounds a bit like the story of the emperor's new clothes. One could get hurt speaking about the "naked" truth.

Also, the Arabic language occurs not in letters, but symbols and characters. Each stands for an experience unique unto itself. One does not add on or delete as is possible in English. The syntax, language patterns, and experiential realities represent distinctive, asymmetrical motifs. The level of communication difficulty increases exponentially as the constructions of reality and linguistic configurations vary widely. It is not hard to grasp how major misunderstandings and misperceptions of threat can occur between such distinctive cultural motifs.

The Islamic perception of the West as infidels (e.g., materialistic, self-gratifying, soul-less beings) reflects the distortions of one cultural motif unable to meaningfully relate itself to another. When Osama bin Laden and his terrorist group misperceived American presence in the Gulf as a violation of holy ground, they misread the material presence that was supportive of the Arabic world as a sign of violation. This only fueled the fires that had already been burning for years. The United States's support of Israel in the Mideast is another source of aggravation to the terrorists (and to a lesser extent the Arab-Islamic region as a whole). It is misperceived as an extension of the West (which in their mind is only the beginning of the West's effort to take over the region). The Islamic fusion of religion and lifestyle, the intense value attributed to experiential sacredness of holy ground in their all-or-nothing construction of right and wrong reality contributes to an accumulation of misperceptions.

The West's motifs of individuality, freedom of expression (especially in material forms), and pragmatic enterprise are all literally foreign characteristics to the motif of Islam. In order to de-emphasize the existence of the infidel, it is imperative for mainstream alternative cultural motifs to evolve derivatives of their central forms that are more moderate. Such moderation would allow for a range of possible derivational forms. The Islamic religion has various formative derivations, previously mentioned, that, while embodying the fusion of religion and lifestyle, offer flexibility into the manner in which that is achieved. The Islamic fundamentalists lack such range and flexibility; that is what makes them so dangerous. Yet, the more the unique, idiosyncratic characteristics of a culture's motif are highlighted and elaborated, the greater clarity and accuracy in perception and understanding.

Terrorism in Islamic fundamentalism is supported indirectly (and at times not so indirectly) by individuals and organizations throughout the world. Many so-called charitable organizations are simply fronts for ways to generate income to fund terrorist activities. While governments can weed these out, getting at the roots of such supply is the most effective. It is not just extremists who misperceive, able only to see the infidel. There are sentiments throughout the Islamic world that unfortunately echo the rigid, stereotyped misperceptions of the West that the terrorists possess. It is the education and elucidation of how unique cultural motifs actually are that is needed to enlighten the populations of these cultures.

Such an enlightenment of the citizenry of both the East and the West can serve to reduce, if not eliminate, those who supply terrorist organizations such as Al Qaeda. Curiously enough, there was a study published about a Harvard University doctor who had discovered how eliminating the blood supply to cancerous tumors in the body would shrink and eventually eliminate the tumor. In a similar fashion, illuminating the general public regarding how unique Eastern and Western cultural motifs actually are in form and content can assist in eliminating the financial supply to cancerous organizations such as Al Qaeda.

The rigid form of Islamic fundamentalism operates not in one specific area or location, but rather in a nonstate, pervasive throughout the world though centralized in Islamic countries. The motif of such a terrorist organization has been likened to a virtual state. This virtual state implies a formlessness of motif as far as any nation-state boundaries are concerned. Therefore, it is an ideological motif involving the spread of ideas and concepts, manifest across groups of collective individuals. Yet, there is no actual country called Al Qaeda, as there is a country called Saudi Arabia. The motif of networks and webs of information connection is more the nature of its formativeness. It is manifest in the form of cells or self-contained autonomous groups of individuals able to act with similar ideas to other cells', yet are self-organizing and purposeful. Its virtuality is its essence of existence. If it had fixed, geographical roots, it could not maintain its mutated form of virtuality. It would then become as vulnerable as every other nation-state (notice how the United States could attack them in Afghanistan). Formative mutations are motifs lacking their own roots for derivation at their current level of evolution. If healthy motifs are nurtured in their ability to develop inherent formativeness, such diversity can weed out unhealthy mutations.

Ironically, there is the same quality characteristic of entities known as fractals. These are mathematical expressions that are self-organizing entities and patterns. They generate replications of themselves in what is called self-similar ways. Motifs themselves have such characteristic qualities.

What this all suggests is that to effectively deal with terrorism both at its roots and its eruption means mastering the unique nature of cultural motifs.

Chapter 7

RESURRECTING UNIQUE CULTURAL MOTIFS: RESOURCES IN HEALING

The need for mastery in cultural motifs is reflected in the root causes of terrorism (Kupchan, 2002). These roots have more to do with coming to grips with the modern world itself than with the West. The sense of poverty and having been left behind in technological and cultural advancements, as well as oppressive governing regimes, contribute to the seeds of terrorism. However, modernity is strongly identified with America and other Western countries. The aftermath of 9/11 seems to have spurred America through the Bush administration to narrowly view developing countries as a potential breeding ground of terrorism. This can be a misguided perception creating a self-fulfilling prophecy. Developing Islamic countries have distressed politics requiring reform of their infrastructure supported by humanitarian aid (Kupchan, 2002). The lack of respect for their cultural, political, and humanitarian condition expressed through aggressive U.S. policies only serves to create pseudogeopolitical fault lines.

The tendency for America to act unilaterally (President Bush's United Nations speech regarding Iraq's potential danger of possessing weapons of mass destruction sent the message that with or without the UN, America would act on Iraq) has become more intense since September 11. While understandable in terms of human psychology, such policies threaten alliances and connections among America's allies. The need to maintain collaborative alliances between the United States and the rest of the world beyond strategic needs and mere lip service is essential to foster conditions that support cultural motifs on a global level. The potential overreaction of the United States, believing that there must now be a new world order, threatens the present nation-state identities of countries and their cultural motifs. Such threatening policies would only exacerbate the seeds of terrorism. The United States is already identified with encroaching globalization threatening both Western and, more severely, Islamic cultures. Escalated unilateralism, where America aggressively accelerates acting on its own in dealing with rogue countries such as Iraq, only serves to destabilize the Islamic region and augment misperceptions of America as imperialistic and imposing its cultural motifs (disguised as democracy and freedom) onto the rest of the world. The recent discovery of North Korea having developed nuclear weapons (when they agreed with the United States to stop all development) makes them more threatening than Iraq. Yet, the focus of U.S. foreign policy is on the lesser threat of Iraq. This further contributes to the perception of the United States as biased against Islamic countries. Despite the despot Saddam Hussein, the perception of the United States as aggressor is reinforced.

Mastering motifs among and between cultures begins with establishing constructive ways of combating terrorists groups (e.g., Iraq) without fueling the already burning hotbeds of Islamic culture that misperceive the West as seeking to dominate and oppress them with Westernization.

To create security in the post–9/11world, the Bush administration has taken on a policy of seeking to bring democracy to the Arab and Islamic world (Garfinkle, 2002). The grand design is to homogenize the Islamic culture with democratic liberalism and, in so doing, enhance nation building and eliminate poverty, which have been the psychological supports upon which terrorism justifies itself (Garfinkle, 2002). While on the surface appealing, the last 30 years of American foreign policy have indicated that real transformation comes from within countries in their own, unique way.

DEMOCRACY PARADOX

There are many problems with this policy of seeking to make a safer world for America through globalization of democracy. First, the initial, transitional phases of installing democracies have led countries becoming more aggressive and warlike. This is especially true in non-Western societies where democracy empowers representative groups to appeal to local ethnic and religious loyalties tending toward anti-Western and thus anti-democratic policies (e.g., in Indonesia, Algeria, and Nigeria).

In addition, hypocrisy of diplomacy would be created by Arab democracy in regard to the ruling-class regimes the United States presently supports (e.g., Egypt, Jordan, and Saudi Arabia). The presence of totalitarian regimes is also symptomatic of the unique non-Western nature of the culture's society. The kind of democracy we enjoy in America requires a certain dispositional character or set of perquisites. Such characteristics include a society's readiness to consult reason in recognizing equality and freedom. Being able to exercise restraint, abide by democratic principles, and avert harm to others' life, liberty, and pursuit of happiness presupposes guidance by reason and law. Democracy may challenge non-Western cultures that lack historical precedence in exercising reasoned restraint under conditions of unbridled freedom.

Prior to World War I, only English-speaking countries and France were democracies (Holland, the Scandinavian countries, and Switzerland had derivative democratic forms). Experiments in democracy after 1919 (e.g., Italy, Germany, Japan, and Poland) ended in disappointment.

The last half of the twentieth century experienced numerous emerging democracies. The post–cold war era has seen a proliferation of democracies throughout many parts of the world. Yet, many of these democracies are derivations from the original motif. That is, they are generally illiberal, or managed, democracies (Garfinkle, 2002). Yet, with the onset of the information age, urbanization, literacy, American magnetism and so forth, there are ever-increasing numbers of democracies that prosper in both economic and political terms (Garfinkle, 2002).

MULTIPLE DEMOCRACIES

Democracy is not a dichotomy of all or nothing. It can exist to varying degrees in various expressions. Many developing democracies in non-Western cultures may be similar to but different from what Americans are familiar with. Elections may be fewer and far between and may be more of a referendum than an actual election. Both pessimists and optimists are uniquely predisposed to what forms and degree of democracy are possible in Islamic countries.

Muslim political cultures are large and diverse. Their diversity is vast, historical, anthropological, and complicated. The Islamic world consists of a venerable civilization beyond a religion. Turkey is the most developed democracy in the Muslim world among the few that exist. The Arabic world lacks any democracy at all.

The prerequisite dispositional characteristics are not present in Arabic societies. For example, they do not believe that their source of political authority is intrinsic (this prevents pluralism and legitimate debate in the culture). The concept of majority rule is unheard of in Arabic society (this prevents the polity from being liberal or free). Finally, there is the rejection that all citizens are basically equal in the eyes of the law (this undermines the foundation of free elections as a principle of government formation) (Garfinkle, 2002).

ISLAMIC MOTIFS

The essential nature of the Islamic motif is in stark contrast to that of Western democracy. For over 1300 years it has adhered to the central principle of divine, extrinsic authority that is indisputable. The absolute quality of this principle stems from Islam as a monadic religion inspired by divine revelation. As its teachings are a direct revelation from Allah, no interpretation or debate of His word is tolerated. This positioning radicalizes the Islamic religion.

Heresy and infidels are perceptions conveyed to any other religious beliefs. Garfinkle (2002) relates the story of an Islamic law professor who explained Islamic tolerance as "well, of course I hate you because you are a Christian, but that doesn't mean I want to kill you." The events of 9/11 demonstrate that fundamental extremists have zero tolerance and mean very much to kill.

The leadership motif in Islam follows from such orientations. As there is only one God who has only one law, it follows there is only one design structure permitted. The caliphate is the one leader with only one accountability (nondemocratic) that is an a priori alignment of religious truth and religious communal will. Governmental concerns are resolved in conversation and dialogue by seeking oneness of consensus among the community. Such unilateral forms of construction and operation are in stark, asymmetrical contrast to Western motifs of majority rule, common-law assemblage (e.g., the United States Congress), and laws (perceived by Muslims) as expedient and secular that deviate from divine law.

The Western motif invokes the principle that truth is intrinsic in society, which is pluralistic and fallible because men are fallible. It is common sense in Western culture that 51 percent means the majority rules. Islamic cultural law perceives such criteria as incomprehensible as this violates their law of 100 percent communal consensus aligned with the one will of Allah.

America grows stronger with diversity and a mosaic of cultural motifs (as long as it does not violate Western principles). The Islamic East has found strength in preventing rifts and dissension, which served to shield and protect them from feudal tribes and uncertainty in their world.

Leadership in America operates on a system of checks and balances (for example, the judicial, executive, and legislative branches of government). Leadership in the Islamic caliphate usually was based on heredity, lineage, and consensus (e.g., of one thought and one mind of one God, or Allah) of community elders (e.g., *ijma*) (Garfinkle, 2002). Ironically, the commonly accepted principle in America of one person, one vote, implies an individual equality that is unheard of in the Islamic culture. The latter mandates inequality because of its template of traditional authority from a hierarchy of lineage traced back to Allah. Thus, men have more rights than women, as does age over youth, and education over peasantry (Garfinkle, 2002).

American women enjoy greater equality and recognition (though this has been and still continues to be a challenge) than their counterparts in the Islamic East. The liberation of women in the Islamic culture has presented a major threat to the male, hierarchical design (as it had to American men in past years, but not to the design structure of the body politic as it has in the Islamic culture).

Western democracy destabilizes Islamic male hierarchy to such an intimidating extent that it could contribute to the radicalization of men into even more traditional, fundamentalist tendencies. Efforts to force, impose, pressure, or otherwise coerce Islamic cultures to accept Western style democracy is likely to result in continued radicalization of the Islamic region (Elliott, 2002).

The imposition of Western motifs of democracy onto Islamic motifs thus rigidifies the formative nature of cultural motifs both in the Islamic theater (with the ensuing backlash from intimidated Muslims) and in American motifs. Witness the unilateral, single-minded focus of the Bush administration after 9/11 to go to war with Iraq. Bush encourages debate and dialogue while he prepares the military and the American people to do battle against one of the triumvirates of his "axis of evil" rogue countries.

There are further implications of motif imposition that create backlash and prevent a resurrection and emergence of cultural motifs. The issue of competing with the West requires the Islamic countries to adopt scientific education, the free flow of information, and the liberation of women into the workforce and to enhance genuine privatization and free trade. Such a challenge is not unlike an American boxing champion challenging a sumo wrestler. Their skills, talents, and ultimately, motifs are vastly different and unique. Their lack of equivalence makes it a contrived, no-win situation.

WHOSE MOTIF IS IT ANYWAY?

One can hardly expect countries of unique cultural orientations of motifs to engage in win-win enterprises if one is compelled to essentially play according to the other's motivation (e.g., motif). The present movement toward globalization involves economic and market considerations that are essentially Western in orientation. From stock markets, multinational companies, advanced technology, to the Internet, these fortes of Americanized modernity are exported to the world at large. It is no wonder that Arabic and Muslim cultures are both envious and resentful, perceiving the West as tempting and simultaneously corrupting. How would we as Westerners fare if we were compelled to adhere to a religious alignment of one-mindedness? What would we experience if required by globalization pressures to place at a premium a oneness of alignment among God, community, consensual validation, political leadership, and corporate America simultaneously? How would present-day corporate America (e.g., Enron, Arthur Anderson, WorldCom, and CEO retirement packages) thrive in such a religious-oriented guidance system?

The point is that it is a mistake for any cultural motif to be expected (and even required by corporate globalization) to compete according to one culture's motif while in the process violating its own unique motif. There is challenge to define, articulate, and resurrect a culture's motif in response to the incursion (no matter what form, economic or military) of another. To this extent, globalization of American modernity is growing, representing a positive challenge to the East. However, if pressed too quickly, disrespecting the unique idiosyncratic nature of Islamic motifs, perilous radicalization into extremist fundamentalism will continue to evolve.

Resurrecting unique cultural motifs means acknowledging cultural differences in operational ways (e.g., defined behaviors). That is, there are unique variances among motifs (as have been characterized between West and East). The differences are more asymmetrical than oppositional in that the design structures are uniquely distinct at different levels of organization. The East operates at a monadic level of unilateral oneness. This is asymmetrical to multicultural diversity that is paradoxically all too American. Pluralism is uniquely Western in that being different means to be "uniquely the same." Such "sameness" is a violation of consensual will aligned with Allah, who is of one mind.

The linguistic characters of the West and its language patterns also are remarkably asymmetrical. For example, in English the phrase "I love you" applies in multiple contexts (e.g., I love my dog, cat, house, car, wife, husband, child, job, etc.). In Arabic, there is only one character symbol for each type of "love," conveying distinctly unique phenomena for each experiential event. They are not interchangeable as in English. Arabic has one character symbol for each life experience. English and other Romance languages have sentence tree structures that allow plugging in, if you will, interchangeable objects, subjects, and adjectives that can convey relatively similar or different meanings. For example, "my dog," "cat," "house," "car," "wife," "husband," "child," "job," etc. are all interchangeable linkages referring to the experience of love. Arabic has nothing like these linkages, but rather character symbols with each dot and character respecting a unique experience in itself (e.g., "I love my wife" has its own symbol, which is not interchangeable and does not allow linkages to rebuild variant sentence design structures).

The Islamic motif of oneness is unique and idiosyncratic to the East and literally foreign to American motifs of thinking and living. There are powerful overlaps, however, between cultural motifs. For example, democratic qualities can exist in variant forms of Arabic and Muslim cultures. The scarcity of such synergistic forms (e.g., interfacing motif deviations of East and West) suggests the need for internal, widespread development of Islamic interests as a prerequisite for democracy to be seriously considered.

Acceptance is the first step to change and transformation. There is a profound need for the West and the East to accept both in word and deed the unique cultural distinctions motifs possess and express. Before 9/11, the East experienced the economic and corporate marketing of American cultural motifs exported to the rest of the world. After 9/11, the East now experiences an acceleration of such exportation with the intensification of military action. While completely comprehensible considering the threat and horror, the long-term consequence of expansive, aggressive, unilateral action of casts America into its own single-mindedness. In this way, it shifts its operating motif closer toward the fixations of Eastern motifs.

EAST MEETS WEST

The war on terrorism invokes a virtual reality where there are no clear-cut boundaries of enemy nation-states. Rather, there is a diffuse spread of a cancerous ideology seeking only to undermine the threat of the infidels.

Curiously, the terrorist assault of Islamic fundamentalists (Al Qaeda and Osama bin Laden) provoked America to become more unilateral in the four to five months after 9/11. While America enjoyed almost worldwide support immediately following the horror of 9/11, it has since found itself becoming more isolated from the international community. The severity of a unilateral America willing to go it alone (e.g., in the case of Iraq, efforts to spread democracy throughout the Islamic region, etc.) ironically mirrors the "oneness" of mind and consensual will of a single-minded community aligned to an absolute authority.

How paradoxical that the emphasis on American motifs that emphasize diversity, majority rule, and competing dialogue can be provoked to behave in simpleminded ways, not unlike the cancerous terrorists. There is an old saying that, whom the gods would destroy, they would first make angry. The United States needs to be careful that it does not become part of the cancerous tumor it seeks to eradicate.

The attack on the World Trade Center on September 11 was an attack on America's way of life both symbolically as well as literally. It was an attack on our motif as a uniquely free and powerfully diverse culture and country. While Americans have been encouraged to continue to live their natural way of life (as natural as one can under the circumstances), this implies combating an ideological motif by strengthening and enhancing our own patriotism and American way of life. The danger is that America could become the very thing it deplores—a single-minded, intolerant, one-willed consensus. If that becomes the case, America could win the battle on the military front but lose the war of motifs in self-destructing its own cultural motif of tolerant pluralism. It would allow itself to be provoked into single-minded unilateralism. Recent ABC News polls (2002) have indicated rising antagonistic sentiments toward Islam. It appears that increasing numbers of Americans are also developing more single-mindedness in their attitudes.

The current state of international affairs is complex and more difficult than ever before. The doctrine of preemption to ward off impending threats before they happen (to prevent another 9/11), while effective in the short run, is tantamount to maintaining a permanent state of war long term. The logical extension of such a strategic positioning requires America to gain total control over all nation-states at all times. Such preventative thinking generates controlling cognitions of single-minded vigilance (forgetting to continually interface with the world community). America can be obsessed (and thereby controlled) by the need for global control (Hassner, 2002).

The complexity of the international community requires multilateral cooperation and institution building (Hassner, 2002). Preemption over the long haul, if left to one country functioning unilaterally, presents a global destabilization of the world community. The irony of America's potential for unilateralism involves an asymmetrical form of rights and duties regarding national sovereignty and international interventionism. In other words, the United States assumes it can both claim for itself absolute sovereignty as well as absolute rights of infringement involving the sovereignty of others.

Adding further to the irony, America refuses to recognize any superior law or authority that might limit the freedom of its own action. This is reminiscent of the Islamic cultural motif of chastising the expediency of manmade laws as not being of true divinity. As a consequence, America's unilateralism begins to converge toward a self-authorization to act in its own behalf, not out of the rule of law (e.g., international law) but rather out of its divine and inalienable rights (God given) to its own survival. Such an alignment is precisely the way Islamic cultural motifs have learned to survive. The battleground of terrorism seems to have leveled the field, where the fundamental survival of formative motifs is now at its most basic level. This is the fundamentalist way of fusing religion, lifestyle, and survival. They are all fundamentally aligned. If we are to defeat terrorism in the long term, do we join them at their level or do as Abraham Lincoln suggested: Make our enemy our friend and challenge him or her to rise to our level, thus preserving our way of life?

Fighting terrorism involves intelligence agencies, targeted military action, world coalitions, and so on. It also involves maintaining and enhancing unique cultural motifs in our and other countries' way of life. Yet, there is a twist in the scheme of things here. While our cultural motif needs to expand and express itself, it needs to do so in ways that respect and enhance the rights of other cultural motifs to behave in similar fashion. Globalization, American style, is overwhelming other cultural motifs, creating dangerous imbalances between America and the international community.

As of this writing (post–September 11), there is a great deal of anti-American sentiment. Some would ascribe this to America being the only superpower left after the cold war. Yet, many of the criticisms have more to do with America's power being so great that it doesn't have to listen to or answer to the rest of the international community. This is evidenced by the unilateralist tendencies of the Bush administration. Even though he did go to the United Nations to appeal for tough resolutions against Saddam

Hussein of Iraq (who has defied 16 United Nations resolutions to date), his attitude before and after his presentations was to go to war with Iraq whether it has arms inspectors or not. While it is essential to disarm Iraq, they have not demonstrated to be any more dangerous now than they were for the past 11 years since the Gulf War. While this particular controversy continues, American efforts to encourage international motif building are waning. Witness the failing follow-through in Afghanistan. After the military operation has subsided, little effort to stabilize and enhance their infrastructure has been sustained.

The whole dynamic economic globalization involves American modernity, which is perceived as an expansionistic imposition of the American cultural motif onto those of the rest of the international community. This is not meant to imply that America should not grow and expand. The point here is that it has not taken into consideration the long-term consequences and impacts of its multinational corporations on the cultural motifs of other countries. When a forest is cut down, new trees need to be planted. America and the international community need to work together in multilateral ways to insure that all of the cultural motifs of each country and civilization are enriched and nurtured.

In America, we have antimonopoly laws to provide fair and equitable competition among diverse businesses (think of the U.S. government versus Microsoft). No one business is allowed to dominate the market. The same principle needs to apply to America and the international community as well.

Chapter 8

REFINING MOTIFS IN CULTURAL PERSONALITY: INSPIRATIONAL DEVIATIONS

In the context of post–9/11, American unilateralism has taken on a deeper, more profound onus of unipolar, global dominance (Tucker, 2002). Vice President Cheney (Tucker, 2002) has espoused a plan for over ten years how the United States should be the dominant world power preempting the rise of any other national power that could be a challenge. The tragic experience of 9/11 has galvanized high levels of vigilance and control to prevent another terrorist attack.

While natural and human, the way a country responds as a whole reflects a kind of collective consciousness or character of that culture. In America, the cultural personality of that character involves responding to grievous loss and pain through characteristic willfulness, taking the course of events into one's own hands, and a tendency to become counterdependent. Such character can be seen in cultural heroes like Rocky, Superman, the Lone Ranger, and the John Wayne and Clint Eastwood tough-minded, independent cowboy. These characters emulate heroic struggles against all odds after having suffered some mortal, life-changing wound. The old saying, "if it doesn't kill you, it will make you stronger," reflects the psyche of the classic American, rugged individualist.

The current Bush administration has expanded its focus from concentrating on the perpetrators of 9/11 (Al Qaeda and Osama bin Laden) to Saddam Hussein of Iraq; the countries of Sudan, Libya, and North Korea; and eventually the world at large. The perception of the Bush administration by one of America's strongest European allies, Germany, is to have compared him (quite slanderously) to Hitler. While the German officials have apologized (as they well should have), it is indicative of the backlash and negativity such a post–9/11 strategy has engendered.

Trauma and shock both on the individual and cultural levels create similar overreactive, regressive, all-or-nothing thinking and anticipatory anxiety. In short, hypervigilance to potential dangers coupled with catastrophic thinking (traumatic effects from 9/11) can result in extreme degrees of defensive and aggressive behaviors.

The preemptive strategy after 9/11 reflects these characteristic dynamics. It is essentially: the best defense is a preemptive offense. At the end of the Desert Storm war in 1991, the United States government (with President Bush, number 41) left Hussein of Iraq in power to prevent the more radical Kurds from taking power. Hussein is a Sunni Muslim, which is less radical than the Shiite Kurds. Now, over ten years later, President Bush, number 43, has reframed Hussein as an immediate and present danger to America and the world.

THE REAL CLEAR AND PRESENT DANGER

Such is the context of seeking to establish and enhance cultural motifs throughout the world. Mark Leonard (2002) has identified the severe lack of public diplomacy—the task of communicating meaningful messages to the public (citizenry) of other countries. He cites the rise of democracy, greater availability to international news, and the emergence of global, nongovernmental organizations (NGOs) as constraining national governments. Popular perceptions, not governments, have set the pace in international diplomacy. This was demonstrated in Kosovo where public opinion could have, if not nurtured, destroyed a powerful coalition. Winning the hearts and minds of the Muslim (and maybe to some extent) American citizenry involves nurturing healthy, meaningful, empathic information of who and what their cultural motifs really are.

The real danger is in a stereotypical, restrictive dialogue that ignores the real descriptive artistry of all cultures. Sadly, after the cold war, the United States suspended both the Voice of America and the United States Information Agency. Other countries mimicked the United States and scaled down their cultural promotions also.

INTRICACY OF CULTURAL MOTIFS

A different form of engagement needs to emerge, not just more information (Leonard, 2002). To get the desired results, it is essential to acknowledge the perspectives, beliefs, and truths that each culture espouses. Whether in human rights or military defense, knowing the unique, idiosyncratic nature of your audience is essential. There also needs to be a two-way dialogue between cultures, not a one-way information flow from West to East (e.g., Britney Spears, Chicago-style pizza, and Coca-Cola). Public diplomacy involves imagination and symbols in communication. As 93 percent of all communication is nonverbal (Leonard, 2002), the cultural dialogue between motifs needs to involve experiential components (e.g., language, visits to other countries, and cultural exchange centers). Cultural motifs are comprehended and dialogued best through the actual relevant experience of unique customs, meanings, linguistic patterns, and rituals of expression.

BATTLE FOR SYMBOLS

The targets of the attacks on the World Trade Center, the Pentagon, and what was intended to be Congress (that is, Flight 93, which crashed in Pennsylvania) are all symbols of American capitalism and governmental centers of power. Tragically, the terrorists' motif of fusing religion and politics in their world directed them to seek to impose their radicalization of motif onto ours. The battleground then is symbolic as well as materialistic. The literal symbolism of the Islamic fundamentalist is this fusion of symbol with concrete reality.

To win this ritualistic war against terrorism is to enrich, paradoxically, the cultural motifs of all countries, not dominate them. It is their perception of having to fight for survival that makes a cornered animal dangerous. The intricacy of motifs is a wonder and it is to such artistry that attention will now turn.

THE EIFFEL TOWER

An obvious cultural symbol is the Eiffel Tower in Paris, France. It was built in 1887 by Alexandre-Gustave Eiffel. Its design is a fascinating merger of designs. At its base, it flares outward into a delta shape. As the structure rises, the four curved legs merge into one column. This column rises to the top, culminating in a capped dome. The merger of shapes and designs reflects the interaction of the delta design at the base (essentially feminine) rising and merging into a columnar-capped dome at the top (essentially masculine). Is it any wonder this symbol serves as a global sign of love for couples the world over?

The motifs of cultures both within and between echoes such interactive flow of one design structure merging into another (as in a dialogue of formative designs). This dialectical flow of formative design structures morphing from one to another and then another taps into networks of global motifs. Such flowing emergence of one formative design structure evolving into various others represents a multifaceted morphing capability of motifs themselves.

Examples of this flowing design emerging, submerging (interfacing or combining with other formative designs as in the Eiffel Tower), and re-emerging into a different unique form can be seen in East-West cultures. As depicted earlier, Islamic culture fuses Allah, religion, and lifestyle into one movement. It is the newest (A.D. 622) (VanBiema, 2002) of the three major monotheistic religions (Islam, Christianity, and Judaism). Muhammad, the Islamic prophet, is viewed as placing a seal on all other prophets as he is the latest to emerge. Islam is the youngest of the three monotheistic religions. It considers the Islamic Koran, with its newer and improved revelations, as perfect and better than the other two religions. Because of its youthfulness, Islam tends to be more idealistic (i.e., inflexible) and literal in its interpretations of the word of Allah (God) (Rammelkamp, 2002).

The motif of literalism reflected in Islam also gains its roots from the Persian culture (A.D. 225–637) and the militant, rigid regime of the Sassanids (Rammelkamp, 2002). The advent of Muhammad and Islam galvanized into an Islamic empire embedded with literal, militant characteristics.

The design structures of the Islamic motif (while variant in modern times) perpetuate versions of literal militants. For example, the striving for jihad (the Islamic term for holy war) is a striving to practice religion in the face of persecution and oppression (Rammelkamp, 2002). This may occur four ways: (1) by the heart (battle of heart over vice); (2) by the tongue (spreading the word); (3) by the hand (acts of good, avoidance of evil); and, (4) war (against non-Muslims) (Rammelkamp, 2002).

Notice how such a motif of Islamic design structures submerges (combines with) those of Christianity of the West. The Bible of Christianity (as well as the Old Testament of Judaism) also reflects the word of God. In the Christian religion, when the priest blesses the wine and bread it has been transformed (literally) into the body and blood of Jesus Christ. There is no symbolism. There is the fusion of physical substance and spirituality into the actual incarnation of Christ the Savior's body and blood. While today many Catholics will describe this symbolically, receiving Holy Communion becomes literally receiving Christ into one's life.

The incarnation of God and man through Jesus Christ is in itself a fusion of religion and material world. When the early Christians gave their lives as martyrs to the lions of Rome, they were embodying the merger of actions in this life to consequences in the next life.

RE-EMERGENCE

Intriguingly, Christianity (especially Catholicism) has re-emerged with less rigid, literal interpretations of how to worship God. For one, Christians no longer have to be eaten by lions to get to heaven. They are not going to burn in eternal damnation if they miss church on Sunday and they won't be punished by God (though can one ever really be sure?) and go blind if they masturbate.

What's happening in Christianity is a formative flexibility of derivational design forms. That is, Christians have more room for personal interpretation on how they choose to uniquely worship God. Yet, with all the changes in the Church, we find horrendous happenings of priests sexually abusing children over past decades. Formative flexibility is one thing, but flagrant disregard for the laws of God (and man) is quite another.

It is at such points that mature religions like Christianity are challenged about their adherence to holy scriptures by the young upstarts of newer religions (e.g., Islam). While the design structures of younger religions tend to be more all-or-nothing, black-and-white (or East and West) in their thinking, they do bring fresh challenge to older religions to renew core ideals but in more mature ways.

DIALECTICAL TENSION

The movement of design structures in motifs to and fro reflects a dialogue or exchange between them. The Western culture with its Christianity has moved into more secular forms of living. Individuation and uniqueness are heavily stressed (e.g., America is a fiercely independent nation). Yet, a nation of individuals, at some point, needs to come together in a united state of individual consciousnesses to move as "one nation, under God, indivisible." Within America and the Western world, we have a constant tension of dialogue (e.g., like an accordion moving in and out) undulating around issue after issue (e.g., Do we attack Iraq? How do we stimulate an anemic economy?).

There is a similar dialectical tension that exists between cultural motifs. While it is wonderful for each person in America to find and express his or her own path to God (or not, as the case may be), Christianity and the culture as a whole may go too far in their deviations from the laws of God (and man). The free love of the 1960s and 1970s has led to many unhealthy and lonely lovers in empty marriages and relationships. This doesn't mean that individual adults shouldn't have responsible freedoms, but where and how do they learn to be responsible if love is free of any effort or learning of self-discipline.

The dialectic of Islamic cultural motifs—rigid, literal, and fused though it may be—is emerging, submerging, and re-emerging with ours in the West. They are flowing to and fro, each formatively shaping and redesigning gradually one another in a constant interplay. There is the saying "to everything there is a season." There is a time to individualize, only to be counterbalanced (perhaps asymmetrically as all motifs seem to be) by alternating levels of juxtaposing design forms. For example, Christianity and the West may benefit to remember and reinvent their core ideals by the exaggerated literalism of Eastern Islamic perfectionism.

The coexistence of East and West does not hinge on finding a solution, but rather on a dialectical tension of morphing cultural motifs that asymmetrically flow between as well as within these (and other) cultures.

THE WOMEN AND THE PROPHET

There are many misunderstandings between the East and the West that dialectical tensions between motifs can clarify. One of the most extreme is the role of women in Eastern and Western cultures. The marked progressive achievements of women in Western cultures are well documented. By the same token, the treatment of women in the East (e.g., especially by the Taliban in Afghanistan) has been deplorable. Yet, little is known of Muhammad's first wife, Khadījah. She was actually an entrepreneurial businesswoman dealing in international trade with caravans. After Muhammad received his prophetic vision, his wife was the first to be converted. She was supported by her husband and played a powerful role in the development of Islam. She continues to this day to be highly revered in the Islamic culture (Pelayo, 2002).

The harsh principles of Islam regarding women do not reflect the actual teachings of Muhammad. Ironically, dialectical interaction with Western cultural motifs accesses latent Islamic core principles lost in its formative years. At its core, Islamic and Christian motifs may share similar seeds of origin though they have sprouted very unique formative derivatives.

INTRICATE ISLAMIC MOTIFS

The design structures of Arabic literature provide revealing insights into their artistic motifs. The Koran was the only book written in A.D. 632 after the death of Muhammad. It required another 100 years for the next two books, grounded in Islamic religion, to follow. These were *The Raids* and *The Life of the Prophet* (Santos, 2002).

These writings set the standard for the literacy structure of future writings. The authors believed that proof and validation of religious events could be substantiated only through narrations from one generation to another. Known as an *isnad* or linked chain (Santos, 2002), the idea was to connect the present author of a written event backward in time to its origin (e.g., to the actual participants or observer of the event). It is similar to what Native American tribes have done, passing down from one generation to the next narrations or storytelling of significant and powerful events over time.

The difficulty occurred when these Islamic stories would become longer and more elaborate. The greater the intricacy of narrated stories, the greater their memory would be taxed. In addition, it was unheard of in Islamic narrations to assume an omniscient point of view of intuiting the thoughts and feelings of people in intricate, historical events (Santos, 2002). As a result, constraints were exerted limiting the range of emotions and thoughts only to those most blatant. Subtle, intuitive elaborations were severely discouraged.

The consequence was a literal, reality-based linkage of narrations devoid of symbolism and richness of metaphor. The irony to these structural constraints is a collection of numerous writings with as many authors known as *Thousand and One Nights* (e.g., *Arabian Nights*). The oldest of these was written in the ninth century known as *The Book of Stories* from the *Thousand and One Nights*. It uses the story of Sheherazade and Dunyazad as a theme through many other tales in the book.

The theme regards Sheherazade using storytelling to delay sexual encounters with an angry and evil sultan. What's fascinating about this book is that Sheherazade does not really tell the sultan stories, but rather relates events that she can link back to reality-based origins. Yet, the whimsical tales embossed with fabulous characterizations distinguish *Arabian Nights*. This is in stark contrast to the reality-based books that are essentially historical, religious, and biographical. Most Arabs today continue to read mainly utilitarian material.

There is a powerful juxtaposition in *Arabian Nights*, which finally was accepted in the Islamic culture in 1950 as a mature work. The content of the stories of Sheherazade is reality oriented. Yet, the context and framework of the tale of Sheherazade and the sultan are fantastical and wondrous. There is interplay or dialectical tension between the reality-based events used by Sheherazade and the fictional confabulations of the tales themselves. The emotional range of personal expression and creative thought is restricted by the constraints of Islamic narration. Yet, there is a need for human beings to innovate and express their uniqueness. The dialectical tension between these polarities creates intricate nuances. That is, concreteness of reality can be so intense and literal as to create a kind of tunnel vision. For example, Sheherazade's relating of events creates a sense of realism in a fictional setting. The dialogue between these contrasting levels of reality can create a magical or illusionary effect of what is or is not real.

As Islam believes in a perfect universe at its origin (e.g., Allah as the prime cause of the universe), narration and linkage are a means of maintaining fidelity with God. Yet, human beings need to diversify and derive their own unique characters. The constraints placed upon people in such contrasting polarities can have curious effects. One is the alteration of reality from a factual basis to one of magic and larger-than-life phenomena.

THE MAGICAL JINNI

The paradox of the Islamic cultural motif is the contrast between (and at times fusion of) fact and fantasy. The artistry of Arabic design structures (e.g., arabesques; geometric shapes; horseshoe arches; lush, woven carpets; and articulated, painted, vined, curvaceous tiles) represents wondrous color and refinement in detail. Many of their tiles articulate complex vines weaving in symmetrical and asymmetrical circles, spirals, and branched derivations (as can be witnessed in the Islamic display at the Louvre museum in Paris). They embody the linear, vinelike connection of roots and origin with articulate, magical, here-and-now manifestations of beautiful characters and beings.

The evolutionary movement of Islamic roots connecting through the intricate, multibranched vines of fantastical gardens captures factual and magical juxtapositions. The interweaving of these themes permeates much of the Islamic motifs.

Fascinatingly, it is also in the Islamic holy book of the Koran. The Koran has devoted a full chapter to what in Arabian mythology is known as the jinni. Western culture is familiar with such creatures known as the magical genie (or jinni) in the bottle (Santos, 2002). There are Muslims who continue to believe in these magical creatures, of which there are five types (all created by Allah from the amorphous fiery origin). These are larger than life (the size of mountains and whose faces can extend over the entire Earth) with supernatural powers and are known as (1) Madrid the powerful, (2) Afreet the intelligent, (3) Sheitan the devilish, (4) Ghillian the shape-shifter, and (5) Jann the least powerful of all.

These fact- and fantasy-based realities are highly contrasted in Islamic motifs, more so than in the West. This is not to say that they could not benefit from more integration and subtle refinement. It is to say that fusion of all-or-nothing juxtapositions is more of a tendency in such motifs. It's sort of a Picasso-like, multifaceted juxtaposition of many front and angular perspectives occurring simultaneously.

It is important to recognize the great minds of Islamic culture dating back to the eighth century (Mondschein & Steinsaltz, 2002). They never questioned their faith in Allah while investigating the world of mathematics, geology, and geography, to list but a few areas. For example, Muhammad ibn Mūsā al-Khwārizmī (A.D. 770–840) made enormous contributions to geometry, astronomy, and geography. His most famous was a treatise, *Kitāb a-jabr wa al-muqābalah*, systematically presented solutions for quadratic equations. The titles *al-jabr* and *al-muqābalah* (meaning "restoration" and "opposition") came to be known as algebra (*al-jabr*) and algorithm (*al-khawarimi*). Faith can be a guide and coexist in a dialectical way with science. Here is a case where origins and manifestations have created beautiful dialogues.

There is a terrible downside to this. When constrained reality (e.g., factual, concrete awareness) is contextualized or framed in extreme juxtapositions (e.g., fantastical states of meaning as in the jinni's lamp), reality becomes dangerously delusional. The results can lead to a devastating dilution of entranced reality states. Witness the horrific events of 9/11 and Atta's message (cited previously) before entering the planes. It was an admixture of reality and entranced distortions.

DIALECTICAL TENSION AMONG MOTIFS: EAST AND WEST

It is critical to grasp the unique characteristic differences between the motifs of the East and West. Like life, this is not something to solve but rather to dialogue and acculturate. Differences imply contrasting (e.g., juxtaposing of each culture's faceted motifs) relationships among East-West motifs. Significant differences do not mean conflict but rather a confluence of ebbing and flowing interaction. For example, the contrasting ebb and flow of an ocean's waves washing upon and receding from a white sandy beach composes a kind of dialogue between the two. The boundary of interaction is energized with vitality and mutual enrichment.

While the ocean enriches the beach with its organic deposits, it is also enriched through the cleansing filters of the sandy beach. Balanced interaction among motifs is everything. While waves may be asymmetrical in form and rhythm, a tsunami can wash away a beachfront as can a polluted beach poison the ocean's water. The differences between beaches and oceans actually serve to define and refine one another through their flowing interactive boundary without which the formative motif of each could not exist and evolve. Far from conflicting and denying one another, the flowing confluence of the beach-ocean dialectical affirms and matures one another in their constructive and formative differences of one another.

One perceives the flowing confluence of differing formative bodies dialectically informing one another in American government. President Bush (representing the executive branch) interactively dialogues his international policies with both Congress (e.g., literally dialoguing mutually defining and refining formative policies regarding the war on Iraq) and the United Nations. While seeking to act unilaterally in his attack on Iraq, he both defines and is defined by the varying formative bodies of government motifs.

The formative position of being president emerges and exists in contrast and in relationship to other branches of derivational government bodies (e.g., the Senate, the Congress, and informally the populace at large). The very formative foundation of the position of president of the United States of America presupposes a United States of America to preside over. Bush as president would be meaningless without other relational, interactive, formative bodies with which to contrast and establish a defining boundary (e.g., a beachhead, if you will).

The point to all this is that no one position can truly act unilaterally without creating a Pyrrhic victory of self-destruction. Not only is this self-evident within the United States of America, it is also self-evident among the countries of the world even though, except for the United Nations, no formal entity like this exists.

The cultural motifs of East and West sometimes are like a bad marriage—can't live with and can't live without. The recent California longshoreman lockout (costing America an estimated billion dollars a day) reflects the remarkable interdependence of America and the world. With shipping frozen at the beachhead in California, products from Asia necessary for American industry (e.g., for automakers and Dell computers) comes to a standstill. In addition, American exports that support U.S. businesses are also dampened. The ripple effect, as it is known, could eventually depress not only American business but world markets overall.

The inseparability of America with the world is not simply a matter of economics, the stock markets, and corporations. The boundaries of nation-states are slowly eroding (like shifting tectonic plates of the continents) into newer formative configurations (Appadurai, 2002). These market-states (e.g., telecommunications) may have similar boundaries as nation-states, but they are more fluid and reciprocally defining on a global level. International corporations interact and dialogue formative relationships with governments across the world. For example, Motorola is dialoguing with Pakistan to install cell phones and other forms of telecommunications in that culture.

The marriage of America with the world is undeniable. We may not like our partners. They may be deadly at times. Yet, we need to know how to dialogue with them to assert a mutually beneficial formativeness in our contrasting cultural motifs. There are mutant offspring that emerge from this marriage. If they are cancerous, intervention at various levels is required (e.g., economic, political, or military). Yet, we can never forget our dialectical motifs. Unilateralism and isolationism risks risk our own Pyrrhic victory of culturally assured motif destruction. The dialectical of East-West motifs emerges in the understanding of formativeness both within our motifs and between them.

PROUD TO BE AN AMERICAN

What does it mean to be American? What is an American? What does one look, act, and sound like? What nationality is American? Where do we come from and how come people from all over the world know an American when they encounter one? The answer to all these questions comes in one word—"mutt"!

The healthier type of dog in the world is the hybrid mutt. While the pure thoroughbred is certainly a work of art, it is the hybrid mutt that is the most resilient, healthy, and multifaceted. How many times have we heard the phrase Heinz 57, following the motif of America's favorite ketchup? American is the free-to-be-me multidiversity of endless ethnicities. The admixture of multiethnic background creates the curious motif of everything, nothing, and one-of-a-kind things. The candor, pragmatism and, at times, shoot-from-the-hip cowboy motif of such hybridism conjures up a kind of stereotype that ultimately does an injustice to being American.

THREE BLIND MEN—ONE ELEPHANT

America is more like the three blind men trying to describe an elephant (e.g., one from behind, from the side, and from the front). America has been and continues to be settled and resettled by wave after wave of emigrants establishing a beachhead in America. The French (who gave us the Statue of Liberty, which we turned around as the arms of the lady who welcomes all), Italians, Polish, Arabs, Asians, and African Americans are all constituent characteristic parts creating the asymmetrical proportionalities known throughout the world as American. The stereotype of "muttism" (and all it entails on the surface) distracts from the rich, cultural mosaic inherently unique to each American. In our desire to fit some American mold, we lose the true masterpiece of complex heritage, our unique motif.

So how do we comprehend the East-West dialectical of cultural motifs? Perhaps it initiates itself in the rich variety America enjoys in its complex hybrid of unique cultural heritage. Compare the varieties of Islamic motifs (e.g., Shiite, Sunni, fundamentalist, Kurdish) with the vast range of hybridism in America. As Muslims draw from a lineage of the past, heritage lines cross, merge, and differentiate. While limited in range, individual Muslims lose a purity of origin, becoming increasingly hybrid. A proliferation of diverse sects subgroupings (including terrorist groups) begins to emerge hybrid forms paralleling America's experience.

ROOTS AND WINGS

America is youth oriented, freedom seeking, and future-is-now designed. Islamic culture as previously mentioned is origin-based in lineage and narration. Yet, Islam is the youngest of the three monotheistic religions (the others are Judaism and Christianity). There are facets of youth that mesh between Islam and America. Both cultures have a desire to grow and prosper. Yet, the contrasts are striking. Islamic culture is oriented toward growing from its origins needing to look backward, staying connected while it looks forward in its evolution. It is like extending roots to grow wings. How does a young child to extend its safety chords from home, enabling it to branch out into uncharted future territory? It needs structure, direction, and safe trial-and-error learning experiences.

MOTIF OF TIME

America and the rest of the West are more future oriented, seeking to find themselves through fulfilling their future potential. In this way, they reveal the nature of their origins. The future unveils fulfillment of what potential was present from the beginning. Time from the past defines the future of Islam. Time from the future defines the meaning of past origins for America and the rest of the West.

These are rather remarkable contrasts that emphasize unique, temporal components of each culture's motif. Ignoring and seeking to superimpose one cultural motif onto another creates fused immobilizations that lead to fixation and destructive dynamics. Witness the ongoing, gut-wrenching carnage of the Mideast, with alternating suicide bombings and Israeli military reaction. Here is a case where the boundary of dialectical tension defines two cultural motifs: not where they cannot live without each other, but rather where they cannot die without one another. It is a sadistic, maddening horror of two cultures exhibiting mutually exclusive terrorism and militarism. They are inextricably intertwined (trapped) in slow, tortured mutual annihilation resulting from the loss of a boundary of mutually defining and refining enrichment. They are like two warring gang members with one set of hands tied together and the other set wielding knives or swords. In mutually excluding one another's motifs, they gradually erode the existence of both. They need that fluid contrasting boundary of ebb and flow coupled with their own respective spatial time zones.

Similar dangers exist at the global level between East and West. Indeed, the Mideast is a holographic, smaller-scale version of similar dynamics that could emerge globally. The motifs of the West, especially in America, exemplify free trade, capitalism, and material accumulation. The motifs of the East reflect the origins of the past as grounded in Allah from whence all material things grow and return. The dialogue between such diverging motifs can interface and flow at the crossroads of how materialism can be used differently for each. The West constantly presses to establish new markets the world over (e.g., Motorola and Pakistan). Yet, the purpose of how Americans and their corporations use telecommunications is quite different from the East. While America constantly presses for new advancements in technology to create market demands, it needs to know when enough is enough for varying cultures. While Pakistan may enjoy the advancements of technology, its use of cell phones and the like may be more grounded in enhancing the connection of the family and religious events and in accelerating information within the confines of traditional lifestyles.

The American version of cell phones, and Europe's, more or less, emphasize the freedom and individual movement they afford people. Similar facets may well apply to capitalistic gains, increasing standards of living in terms of housing and product availability. For example, Iraq, despite the embargo on products since the 1991 Gulf War, enjoys many brands of goods and services similar to those in the West (e.g., their stores stock as many brands of shampoo, conditioners, etc. as American stores). However, their lifestyle of clothing, religious rituals, and ways of using hair products are all in keeping with their cultural roots of motif.

It is a mistake to assume that if Islamic countries use our products, listen to our music, and watch our movies, that they would or should think and be like us. This is the ebb and flow of interfacing facets of our contrasting cultural motifs. It is not unlike two travelers passing one another at a crossroads. They may temporarily share the same point and place in space-time, but they are moving in varying directions to each other. They may greet, share amenities, and make nice, but each has his own path or motif to guide him. Attempting to insist or pressure travelers on differential paths to follow another's motif is to ignore Henry David Thoreau's principle that "each must move to the beat of a different drum." If we can be open to innovative and creative ways in which facets of differing cultural motifs may harmonize, we can discover dialectical boundaries of mutual reinforcement. Curiously enough, East-West motifs have many dialectical facets (they do not have to be, nor should they be, identical to coexist). For example, the power of storytelling and myth is colorful and plentiful in both cultures. They both share a fierce belief in traditions of religious services (e.g., going to church services in the mid-twentieth century was just as intense as going to mosques). There is also nobility and honor in their warriors' fighting for a higher power (i.e., Allah). Family and children are both highly prioritized in each culture. Yet, there are also critical differences reflecting unique motifs. For example, in Arabic families the children grow up to support the family. One would expect this from a cultural motif that stresses the origins of time (e.g., parents as the origination of children reflecting the roots of Allah). Contrast children raised in America and the West, which encourages the children to move out and onward, free to live their own lives. This is consistent with a cultural motif that stresses future time where children are to fulfill their potential (and in so doing fulfill their parents as originators of offspring).

Notice that value judgments of style or motif are more just or correct depending (as Einstein would say) on your relative (relatives are important) position in space and time, that is, your motif. The metaphor of travelers passing at the crossroads is relevant here. Both cultural motifs prioritize families but construct and design their formative direction in remarkably unique ways consistent with cultural motifs.

The danger of radicalizing and prejudicial judgmentalism reflects fixation and rigidity of stunted motifs. When the East or the West view one another as the infidels, the loss of dialectical boundary flow becomes evident. Avoiding fixations and maintaining a dialectical flow that compares and contrasts unique cultural motifs require the respectful recognition of the idiosyncratic uniqueness of motifs in themselves.

WEST WING AND EAST ROOT

The dialectical flow of formative design structures was previously described concerning the Eiffel Tower. In a similar fashion, the narrative lineage of the East's roots interactively flows with the West's wings. Curiously, the popular television show known as *The West Wing* refers to the office of the president of the United States. The symbol of America is the bald eagle. The very spirit and power of America is rooted, if you will, in these eagle's wings.

By the same token, the East's rootedness in its lineage of past narrations anchors it to historical validation. In drawing strength and succor from deep roots, it can grow, branch out, and spread its wings. Islam is invested in its lineage of narrative, historical connection of Allah and the prophet Muhammad. Its focus on maintaining deep-rooted connections fosters its inadvertent outward branching. As vines on scaffolding, past narrations extend out into the future to build on formative motifs of the past. Yet, the focus is linkage to the past not progress in the future.

America (and the West) is invested (or anchored) in the future-is-now aspect of postmodernism. Its focus of maintaining fulfillment of creative potentials in the future inadvertently fosters revisiting its origins in the Constitution and its founding fathers.

There is a dialectical flow of roots and wings that serves as a common ground of growth for both the motifs of the East and the West. The East's allegiance to its literal religious origins requires all future growth to be aligned with its past. It selectively digests and integrates from the postmodern world key characteristic features that maintain this alignment. For example, its news media uses the advanced technology of satellite broadcasting. However, its programming is traditionally aligned with the origins of its religion. The West may call this censorship. Yet, we forget that in our own way, our use of movie-rating systems is designed to maintain family values (which are our origins).

The West's allegiance to its fierce independence requires all past connections to be strengthened and reaffirmed. Notice that the higher the skyscraper (e.g., Chicago's Sears Tower), the deeper the foundation must be
(e.g., multiple basement floors under ground level) to support it. Whether
passing a piece of legislation or raising a child, new laws and child development require learning and aligning with the past to build on for the
future. Change and transformation are based on what came before it, indicating what the necessarily new cutting-edge innovations must be. To craft
and fashion something new requires a leap from somewhere (past) to
somewhere (future).

THE CULTURAL ARROW OF TIME'S MOTIF

One might comprehend the motifs of the East and West through the use
of timelines. A timeline depicts the movement or direction of time (e.g.,
the rate of change or length of interval between events). A curious way to
conceptualize time as it is construed in motifs of East and West is to imagine which end upon which to place God.

Allah (i.e., God) is placed on the original point of time (the beginning)
for the motif of the East. In other words, Allah is in the beginning of
time. The arrow of time points to the past for the cultural motif of the
East. The West does, of course, acknowledge God as the creator of the
universe but focuses upon fulfilling the potential of what God placed in
us to fulfill in the future. Therefore, the God of the West sits on the future
end of timeline.

In a curious way, the cultural motifs of East and West phase in and out
of one another, as do the design structures of the Eiffel Tower. They are not
in conflict but rather in confluence with one another, creating a larger
whole. The ebb and flow of these divergent arrows of time in cultural
motifs reflect the artistic triumph of global motifs working in synergistic
harmony.

It is essential to realize the unique creations emerging from integrating
facets of cultural motifs. If Allah sits at the beginning of time for the East
and God sits at the end of time for the West, then both serve as pillars of
the temple (e.g., humankind's temple). If they are too close or too far
apart, the universe (as humankind knows it) will end (e.g., What is
Armageddon?). Curiously, Kahlil Gibran, in his writings of *The Prophet,*
applied this metaphor to marriage. Perhaps it also applies to the dialecti-

cal flow between cultural motifs, arrows of time, and East-West cultural formativeness.

The following chapter refines and develops the dialectical process of synergistic motifs incorporating critical essentials of religion, God, and formative cultural motifs.

Chapter 9

TRANSFORMATIVE CULTURAL PERSONALITIES AND EVOLUTION

The transformative potency of cultural motifs lies in their efficacy for synergy. As presented previously, interactive cultural motifs asymmetrically (partial congruence or matching) join and merge with one another. Nurturing and maturing them involve honing and pruning (as one would a bonsai tree). The more mature and evolved a cultural motif, the greater its capacity for tolerance, resilience, and creative performance.

The American cultural motif of freedom and opportunity for all has dramatically evolved from the 1960s to the present. Issues of civil rights, feminism, and multiculturalism have made great strides in America partially as a consequence of the growing pains of its cultural motif. American citizens are vastly more informed, open-minded, and resilient to a multitude of social, cultural, and political issues. The value of honing, pruning, and maturing a culture's motif has far-reaching benefits.

Competition, struggle, and conflict are not new to the world. Those cultures that survive have learned to evolve their cultural motifs into highly complex, synergistic, formative societies. The thousand-year prominence of the Roman Empire is a classic example. Its fall came in part because of its loss of contact with its roots and sense of origin.

America has evolved as the most powerful country in the present-day world. Being number one is a double-edged sword. The benefits are obvious. The downside is that we become the number one target of competing cultures. The illusion of isolation and unilateralism has been diminished, but not altogether eliminated for the social-cultural scene. The American culture of the Lone Ranger, the cowboy (e.g., what state does our president come from and what's his motif?) continues to persist (Appadurai, 2002).

America culture has been described as a bull in a china shop. Much of the hostility America and much of the West engender from the global community is because of the one-way direction of cultural flow. Other countries absorb our music, style of clothes, language, and even philosophy of business to some extent. Yet, little of other countries (e.g., Middle or Far East and third world countries) flow in return (Hassner, 2002).

America is probably the largest benefactor to the rest of the world, especially when it's in need. Yet, foreign-aid policy continually needs to learn that struggling countries (e.g., many Arab-Muslim economies) need more than just financial or material aid.

FORMATIVE WORLD OF BELIEF, ART, AND CONSCIOUSNESS

Muslim countries need to enhance and mature the formative consciousness of their countries' cultural motifs. Fundamentalism flourishes in the stagnation of cultural paralysis. Whether self-imposed by historical perspectives or the overwhelming sense from the one-way cultural flow of the West, it is essential that Muslim cultural motifs be matured and evolved.

What contributes to perceived threats of the West by the East is its inherent stagnation and cultural throwback experience to historical times that prevents evolution of their own sophistication. They simply cannot keep pace with the postmodernism of the West. The terrorist Mohammed Atta, who led the 19 henchmen in the September 11 attack, was himself stagnant in evolving in his own culture. This is no justification. To prevent and ensure the future safety of America and the global community at large, cultural maturation of motifs is a critical component toward this end. Yet, this must respect the unique pace and idiosyncratic nature of each culture's motif.

CULTURAL MATURATION OF MOTIFS

The motifs of Muslim culture involve more than achieving degrees or increasing financial income. The artifacts of a culture, its mosques, language, style of dress, sacred days of worship (e.g., Ramadan), and the ways it construes its holy scripture (e.g., Koran) convey symbolic meaning and purpose to everyday life. The evolution of Muslim motifs needs to be viewed with respect and value by America and the West. There needs to be a shift toward two-way cultural flow or at least an effort toward some asymmetrical balance (Hassner, 2002).

The dialectical flow between East and West has demonstrated a rich, tolerant, and interactive flow in Muslim Spain of the fifteenth century. Christians, Jews, and Muslims lived in remarkable harmony and mutual acculturation (Gilman, 2002). While the East has an arrow of time focused toward historical roots, as long as it can retain lineage, it can extend, branch, and in a word, evolve. We in the West are more comfortable leaving the past behind for a better future. However, the cultural motif of the East needs to reaffirm and maintain its anchors (roots) of the past so that it can extend and mature its motifs into the future. The rate of change that the West and America is accustomed to varies asymmetrically to that of the East. As previously described, change is a somewhat foreign concept as the universe already is perfect (vis-à-vis Allah made it so). How the West frames and fashions its concepts, constructs, and constraints (e.g., motifs) in regard to the East is in itself an act of artistic crafting and fashioning. It needs to be remembered that maturing cultural motifs involves expanding, differentiating, and designing innovative evolutions. This is not necessarily done at the governmental level but rather at the level of the culture's citizenry.

THE CULTURAL PERSONALITY OF EVOLVING MOTIFS

The construct of cultural maturation involves developmental principles where one stage builds upon another. As rings of a tree develop layer upon layer as it matures, so a cultural motif differentiates complex layer upon layer. The human brain preserves its ancestral, reptilian origins, yet with evolved additional layers of mammalian and neocortical levels. Cultural motifs also build layer upon layer of increasing levels of differential complexities. The European culture has evolved over many hundreds and thousands of years from tribes within a regional domain to nation-states of ever-sophisticated refinement and artistry to its current euro-communal status.

This latter status bears further exploration. In order for the European Union (as typified by the common monetary denomination known as the euro) to come into existence, its individual nation-states had to evolve to some minimal level of sophistication. War-torn Europe, the setting for two world wars, has now evolved its individual nation-states (e.g., France, Germany, and Spain) toward an integrated, self-identity level unthreatened by this union. Rather, the internal maturity of identity recognizes interdependency needs as mutually enhancing. It is not that they never existed, it is that they were not developmentally ready.

INTERNAL CHARACTER OF CULTURAL MOTIFS

What contributes to this internal character building of cultural motifs is the constant working and reworking of its unique characteristics. That is, as countries such as France and Germany flexed and exercised their respective cultural characteristics (e.g., the world wars, economic and artistic challenges, and adapting to changing world orders), they were compelled to define what they were (and what they were not). France stood its ground taking pride in its unique avant-garde artistry (e.g., angular, precise forms with embellished curvatures and grand architectural landscapes of palaces and monuments). Germany exalted in its reichs of power, boldness, and strivings for superiority. In the end, they both now have honed and pruned their accentuations, developing closely shared boundaries. From Napoleon to Hitler, France and Germany have preserved what is healthy in their cultural motifs, releasing in a mature fashion eccentricities of a Pyrrhic nature.

Theirs and other countries in Europe share multiple borders (e.g., France is bordered by Spain, Switzerland, and Germany). The boundaries are not hard and fast as the interactive dialogue between them create a range of influence. As the waves of the ocean move to and fro on a beach, the shoreline is not a rigid boundary but is a reflection of a range of movement between the rising and lowering tides of the ocean upon the beach.

The same is true with the shared boundaries of France with Germany and France with Spain. The east border of France shared with Germany involves French-speaking Germans, giving rise to beer stubes and eating German sausage. Similar multicultural overlaps are interactively dialogued, if you will, at its boundaries with Spain and Switzerland, respectively.

THE CULTURAL MOTIF OF "MUTT"

Such multiboundary sharing encourages interactive dialogues among Europeans to speak multiple languages. This intermixing creates hybridlike (known as a multicultural "mutt" in America) blends or derivations (known as evolved offspring of parent motifs). These new hybrids are evolved motif figures compared against the larger cultural ground (as in figure-ground contrasts) of each country. It is this hybridism between and among cultures that evolves them into higher ordering, differential formative motives. Just as a cockapoo is neither a pure cocker spaniel nor a poodle, a French-German boundary citizen interacting in the range of cultural boundary overlap is neither pure German nor French. Rather, this citizen is a cultural hybrid of a higher formative order.

Maturation of cultural motifs can occur through interactive reworking of unique characteristic features. In other words, whether the dialectic movement occurs within (intra-active) or between (interactive) cultural motifs, maturation becomes possible.

UNIONS OF STATES AND STATE OF THE UNION

The United States of America and the British Commonwealth (England, Ireland—though not all of Ireland, Scotland, and Wales) are examples of states that have evolved into unions. In turn, there is a higher ordering (groupings of integrated groupings) of these unions into what is known as the state of the union themselves. The evolution of such hierarchies approaches a structural integrity of globalization (VanBiema, 2002). The essence of such evolution is not necessarily a function of economic markets but certainly that is a contribution.

FORMATIVE GEOGRAPHY AND STATES OF UNION

Curiously enough, what all three of these states of union have in common are their geographical constraints. European Union countries are all conjoined on the same landmass (continent). The British Commonwealth loosely approximates this also. Notice that Ireland, being a physically separate landmass from England, experiences conflicted, unstable alliances with the commonwealth. The United States of America clearly is constrained (and therefore bordered) by the American continent (save for Alaska and Hawaii).

The formativeness of geographical design structures clearly affects those of a political and cultural nature. Formativeness operates at multiple levels. When in balance (i.e., healthy), the sharing of boundaries and cultural motifs can mature.

GOLDILOCKS AND THE THREE MOTIFS

Maintaining healthy, shared borders within a continental landmass, which geographically forms the domain of interactivity, can be quite a balancing act. Boundaries too close (e.g., where the overlapping, interactive dialectical is intrusive) can be exemplified by the Mideast conflict. Instead of sharing boundaries creating a range of interactivity, the overlap is so intrusively disruptive as seemingly engulfed in one another's territory. The Palestinians have never really acknowledged the boundaries of Israel, and Israel perceives boundary extension as a justifiable consequence of self-defense. The resulting ongoing carnage of lost lives is the tragic consequence of mutually intrusive borders impairing dialectical maturation of cultural motifs.

The cultural collision of warring motifs concerning terrorism reflects an absence of shared borders. Known as disengagement, the form of terrorism being fought lacks any definite boundary. As Islamic fundamentalists are not set in any one country, they have been described as a virtual state of formativeness (Bobbit, 2002). What this means is the complete collapse of any set physical border constrained by landmass separations. Notice that Great Britain is separated from the European continent via the English Channel. England has refused to use the euro both to protect the pound and concurrently their cultural identity.

Islamic fundamentalists have no landmass constraints to give them formativeness. Rather, they rely upon a more fluid, amoeba-like changeability, forming operative "cells" capable of acting independently of one another and in multiple settings (or landmasses). What contributes to its formativeness is how it derives a hybridlike ordering of its own. That is, it draws its extremist configurations (as well as vast sums of money to fund its worldwide network) from fringe elements existing in multiple countries. Just as it draws income from so-called nonprofit organizations and the sympathies of various countries, it cultivates its aberrant ideology from the disaffections of other Islamic peoples. By concentrating complaints, conflicts, and negativity drawn and collected from the more general Islamic population, it intensifies fundamental extremism worldwide. It is similar to multiple streams of waste materials coming from various neighborhoods, pouring into a common pool of toxic-waste products.

This formative intensification of variant distortions culminates into an aberrant hybrid of what might be considered concentrated evil. Yet, there is no set time or place from where this amoeba-like form of concentrated negativity permanently remains. There is no opportunity for a dialectical interaction of two or more cultural motifs to occur, as there is no shared boundary in which to engage. Drying up and out the funding and multiple cultural disaffections that flow into such an amorphous (but still formative in its own way) pool of waste is definitely a means whereby such terrorism can be rendered ineffective. For such a drying out of resources to occur, nurturing and maturing cultural motifs that do share a common set of boundaries is a powerful necessity. Finding just the right balance of sharedness between cultural motifs becomes just the right porridge that the Goldilocks of the world need.

BUILDING A SHARED BORDER

There is no real natural geographical constraint or landmass design that formatively interacts the East and the West. As a consequence, there is a need to constructively bridge this gap where motifs of each culture mean-ingfully interact, identifying differences as well as similarities. Emphasis is on how each cultural motif is unique. Efforts must be made to avoid stripping and deconstructing what makes the cultural motif unique. This would be tantamount to annihilating what sustains its specialness. Expo-sure of populace drawn from the East and West in designed exchange pro-grams articulating the unique artistry of each culture's motif is one of many methods. All too often, such programs lack the articulation and attention to artistry inherent in cultural motifs. The building of shared bor-ders may develop through meaningful global projects beyond simple cor-porate expansion. The international space station is one such enterprise that builds a genuine, cosmic bridge of multiple, shared cultural motifs. Seeking meaningful collaboration between the East and the West beyond times of simple expediency plants the seeds of global fruition.

UPROOTING EFFECTS OF ECONOMIC GLOBALIZATION

Worldwide markets of globalization and advancing technology have pressured cultural motifs around the world to change and evolve. Yet, very little emphasis is placed on the human factor as it interfaces with advanced technology. The pressures to keep abreast of advancing technology, shift-ing world markets, and global economies threatens to uproot to varying degrees cultural motifs. Even in the United States, that acceleration of technology and concomitant lifestyles challenges relationships, families, and emotional-cultural balances.

If America is feeling the massive impact of these global changes, imagine how threatened and overwhelmed the rest of the world must be. There is much talk of how 65 million years ago an asteroid destroyed the dinosaurs. Rapid globalization pressuring premature growth of cultural motifs could be the asteroid of human life as we know it.

Threats of Iraq seeking to go nuclear, Korea recently announcing it has continued its nuclear program of developing fissionable material, and fears of Al Qaeda gaining access to dirty bombs are all indicators of potential asteroids in the future. The time to begin pacing the maturation of motifs is now, and the emphasis needs to be as much on citizenry as it presently is on governments. There is a need to cultivate, nurture, and respect the unique set of characteristics of each country's cultural motifs. Rather than letting economic and market pressures be the driving priorities, respect and attention to preserving the unique characteristics of a country's cultural motifs need to be in the forefront. Only through pacing the maturation of motifs will there be deep roots to supplant the spreading wings of great, worldwide prosperity. Instead of only a few countries prospering at others' expense, global attentiveness to nurturing cultural motifs will provide greater balance and stability to sustain ever-greater wings of prosperity.

EIFFEL TOWER: SYNERGY, MOTION, AND MOTIF

Cultural motifs refine and mature one another through dialectical synergy. The interacting shapes and forms that flow up and down the Eiffel Tower in Paris exemplify such. As described previously, the singularity of the tower's peak flows downward, spreading into angular quadratic rectangles at the base. Multiple interweaving, latticelike iron curvatures adorn its flowing surface interface. Formativeness evolves as intricate design structures flow into varying asymmetrical shapes and forms. The motif of the tower consists of multiple embedded motifs, each contributing to the existence and meaningful presence of the other.

Interdependency of international cultural motifs shapes, forms, and influences one another through remarkable synergy. American artists present fascinating multisensory exhibits in Paris's museum of modern art (e.g., Mathew Barney). Chicago imports French architecture, enriching entranceways of its mass transportation system (e.g., French wrought iron gateways on Chicago's Michigan Avenue). American foreign policy on Iraq presses for immediate action and unilateralist influencing while being influenced reciprocally by the United Nations Security Council (which includes China, France, and Russia) advocating multilateral action. America challenges the United Nations Security Council to act, and reciprocally, the Security Council challenges America to constrain itself into an integrated multilateral coalition. Each policy reciprocates a formative shaping and designing of the other's motif. In such a way, the synergetic process of honing, pruning, and refining emerges a higher ordering of policy maturation.

The organizing capacity of cultural motifs into higher-order hybrids of refined differentiation is the hallmark of the maturation process. Meaningful enhancement of such processes stems from recognition, respect, and realignment of cultural motifs as interdependent processes of a country's culture and not necessarily of its government's political party at any given moment. For example, while a majority of Americans may favor war against the dangers of Iraq's government, over half of the population prefers it to be a multilateral not unilateral action. Intriguingly, the seeds of one formative motif (e.g., the sentiments of the United Nations) are embedded in the design structure of the other (e.g., the preferences of the American population).

Such a principle seems to hold for many cultural motifs only superficially. For example, the Islamic fundamentalists are extremists (i.e., cancerous) derived from the larger motif of Islamic culture and religion. The motifs of moderate Islam have seeds of Western motifs within them. Not only are there constructs of monotheism, commandment-like principles, and religious rituals (e.g., what is the Catholic Church without rituals?), but also there is a focus on family, lineage, and a historical arrow of time that reciprocates Western religious motifs of needing roots, connection, and continuity of structural values (e.g., family values and traditions). As in the flowing formative design structures of the tower in Paris, the hybrid of these cultural motifs can emerge into an international global work of artistry as synergy in motion matures cultural motifs.

BUILDING BONDS OF CULTURAL BOUNDARIES

The value of authentic diplomacy engages cultures (e.g., East and West) in dialectical tensions (contrasting motifs) synergizing bonds of interactive maturation. The construct of speaking to the public of a country's citizenry uses what is known as soft power (Leonard, 2002) as a means of creating dialectical interactivity and meaningful formativeness between cultures.

Presentation of a culture's motif in the expression of authentic ideas, concepts, and truth engenders trust and meaningful engagement of contrasting motifs. Achieving such authenticity involves presenting a comprehension of how unique the subtle nuances and facets of a culture's motif actually are. For example, the French language, architecture, and style involve a distinctive cut, angle, and intensity. Pronunciation has a distinctive flow that ends with an abrupt cessation. Americans can easily misinterpret the intonation as possible rudeness or disdain when in fact it is part of France's distinctive artistry. For example, vowel pronunciation is at a higher pitch, creating distorted perceptions of attitudes (e.g., aloofness). The Islamic language also has unique, distinctive syntaxes where each experience is represented by only one Arabic character. In the West, words can be coupled and uncoupled interchangeably without altering the essence of the experience.

Americans are accustomed to plenty of room and space, which sustains their unique motif of freedom, choice, and individual expression. When Americans travel to Europe and the East, they experience small hotel rooms, small cars, and small roads (but large expenses). This can create a sense of being shortchanged in not getting the "big bang for the buck." To the citizenry of the East, Americans can be misperceived as intrusive, occupying more than their fair share of space and time available and domineering in their attitude. Interestingly enough, this is exactly the misperception Muslim extremists have protested against in their jihad against the West. References to United States military bases in their Holy Land and undue cultural influences bespeak of such misperceptions of American intentions.

There is effort required to identify the subtle, unique nature of cultural motifs. The investment is well worth the effort when it means preventing bloodshed and terrorist threats. When interviewing Americans living in England (America's strongest ally), many have commented on how difficult it is, at times, to break into the good-old-boy stiffness of the English. It is important to understand that cultural motifs have their own unique logic (e.g., psychocultural logic). The experiences of these Americans need not be taken personally as they are only a sign of the unique syntax and synergistic, idiosyncratic nature of self-organizing motifs. Instead of complaining how their cultural motifs conflict with ours, we need to discern their unique, characteristic nature so as to discover ways of respectfully interfacing with them. When Americans travel to a foreign country, they need to remember they are foreigners to the host country they are visiting. What is required is a mutual, reciprocal effort of translation and reorganization of how each person's cultural reality is constructed. In this way, the foreign element can be reduced between countries and their cultures.

TECHNIQUES OF DIPLOMACY

The concept of soft power requires building deeper relationships for authentic public diplomacy. Presenting accurate information and familiarity of one's own cultural motif to the public of other countries engenders trust and authenticity (Leonard, 2002). Updating information on essential issues, even when not favorable, fosters a sense of integrity and genuineness. The image of a culture needs to be congruent with its actions as a nation. Engaging the populace of other countries through tourism, academic and professional learning programs, product development and so on contributes to building accuracy and integrity of a culture's motif.

Influencing the behavior of other countries toward one another involves encouraging appropriately paced, nonoverwhelming corporate investments (e.g., Motorola in Pakistan, mentioned earlier) that nurture public support for each country's position. In this way, meaningful allies are developed, as there is cultural interfacing and dialogue (e.g., shared product services) that extend beyond simple financial concerns.

Leonard (2002) cites three dimensions to achieve goals of public diplomacy. The first involves the day-to-day news cycle of a country's current events. For example, the outbreak in Britain of foot-and-mouth disease and France's political upheaval of conservative right-wing party candidate Le Pen were clearly and accurately presented to the world as current events within these countries. Such candor and honesty encourages the global community to trust the quality and integrity of how each operates and manages itself.

The second dimension involves a common strategy of how to work with and administer the breadth of how a country and its cultural motif are perceived. Development of a set of comprehensive messages (Leonard, 2002) and planning a series of symbolic and meaningful cultural events reaffirm an accurate depiction of a culture's motif. Cinematic and other photographic events can also clarify the essence of a culture's motif in real-world comprehension.

Finally, developing lasting relationships with a country's key cultural figures (e.g., through scholarships, exchanges, training, seminars, conferences, and access to media channels; Leonard, 2002) maintains longevity and stability in cultural refinement. Establishing peer groups cross-culturally (e.g., political and academic, special activity, and business peer groups) further plants lasting roots of cultural development and differentiation.

Leonard (2002) indicates that presentation of authentic information regarding public diplomacy needs to meet four challenges. The challenges are to: (1) define the target audience, (2) confront hostility toward the West, (3) engage people emotionally, and (4) prove relevance to the public concerned. It is important to identify the parameters of who one's target population is to be. The characteristics and limitations to be employed depend upon the desired outcome of what a country's message is to be. Specific facets of a culture's motif may need to be clarified to one segment of a population more than to another.

The confrontation of hostility to the West can be reduced by a two-way flow of cultural communication. Not only is it critical to have an influx of American culture (e.g., Tom Cruise, Britney Spears, rhythm and blues music, videos, etc.) pouring into other cultures, it is essential to be open and receptive to the predisposing idiosyncratic characteristics of other cultures in return (e.g., European and Arabic music, cinema, fashions, architecture, etc.). Nye (1990) describes how the British portrayed themselves as receptive to other cultures through the use of visual art programs. He cited how America used videos depicting Muslims assimilated into American society while failing to reflect the preservation of distinctive Muslim community life.

The quality of communication conveying essential qualities of a cultural motif requires sufficient sensory and emotional experiences. As 93 percent of all communication is nonverbal, imbuing messages with situations and events evoking sensory (e.g., visual, auditory, kinesthetic) and imaginative, emotional experiences actualizes these nonverbal potentials. Symbolism is another modality that was effectively employed after 9/11. Obvious emotional images influenced people's responses to arousing messages (e.g., Tony Blair standing steadfast with George Bush and playing the "Star-Spangled Banner" at the changing of the guard at Buckingham Palace). In demonstrating support for America, Britain experienced deep affection from the people of the United States.

The authenticity of cultural messages needs to go beyond superficial propaganda and party politics. The diplomacy of the United States understandably places its own interests first. The paradox is that if it is consistently perceived as altering its communications to serve its own interests (e.g., spinning or reframing messages) and not seeking unbiased objectivity, it will lose validity. The need to establish a niche where validity of information is reliable can be seen in the case of Norway. Norway has carved out a valid niche or place of recognition as peacekeepers by employing methods such as foreign aid and conflict resolution that focus on such areas as the Middle East, the Oslo accords, Sri Lanka, and Colombia.

MESSAGES AND MOTIFS

Whatever means of diplomacy are used, it is essential that they capture the uniqueness of a culture's motif. Many Westerners do not grasp the reality constructions of the East's unique motif. Because the West has a future focused, scientific-progressive orientation, it encounters confusion and dismay at what motivates Eastern Islamic countries. Discerning a more refined articulation of their motif may contribute toward greater clarity.

Studying the artistic artifacts and tapestries of Arabic culture at the Musée de l'Institut du Monde Arabe in Paris reveals many facets of their unique motifs. For example, stone fragments with Arabic characters inscribed, picturesque tiled mosaics, and richly colored tapestries all reveal similar motif characteristics. There are high-density concentrations of Arabic symbols and intricate design patterns packed together. For instance, Arabic characters are in the form of miniature sequences tightly situated together in linear fashion. Each line of sequences is evenly layered upon one another like stacked railroad ties. There are no frames or boundaries to their picturesque scenes. Rather, their mosaic tiles merge together into organic living scenarios of trees, people, and animals. Up close, the tiles are separate and distinct from one another though they too are tightly packed together. Superimposed upon the tiles are design colorations that emerge into whole images as if projected onto the tiles.

The scenes are intricate and elaborate, filling up the entire tiled palette. Yet, one gets the impression that the scene extends far beyond that tiled mosaic upon which it was painted. There are no frames to delineate or contain the scene. Rather, the scenario appears to extend far beyond what is visible. The only boundary available is the right-angle, columnlike geometry that reconfigures the Arabic symbols from one level to another. Everything interfaces as facets of a prism through which light is refracted into its multicolored spectrum. There are boundaries only through one set of concentric circles interfacing those that lie below and above them.

The repeating sequences of Arabic symbols closely packed operate as light bands of a prism. Rows and tiers of intertwining loops weave throughout as branches of trees tied in sailor's knots. The design patterns sequentially repeat in a similar but varied asymmetry. There is something new in each repetition, yet the general design structure is relatively consistent.

Such a motif reflects what is known in mathematics as a fractal or in chemistry as a polymer. Both exemplify qualities of self-organization and self-similarity. These are also characteristics of DNA molecules. Curiously, Arabic sculptures build upon themselves in a cylindrical, layered fashion that spirals upward into a domed peak at the top. The DNA molecule has been called the spiral helix, which is also has a cylindrical design structure.

MOTIF IN A NEW LIGHT

The unique features of Arabic motifs in art have far-reaching implications in their social, political, and religious dimensions. To understand this, it is best to draw upon the Islamic tapestry. These tapestries have precisely the same characteristics as do the other artifacts previously described. They have a variety of uses, including at funerals. The tapestry has multifaceted, sequentially repeating patterns in both leveled and layered design. That is, not only are the layers vertical and horizontal, but there is also a third dimension to them (even in a two-dimensional format). That is, there appears to be second ordering of patterning superimposed over the surface or primary level. What this does is create a depth dimension.

Such a dimension in Islamic religious terms is deemed a doorway or portal into another domain (i.e., the spiritual). Indeed in mosques, tapestries are pointed in the direction of the light emitted from lamps symbolized to be brilliant stars. The tapestry is pointed toward the light and thus a doorway or portal is revealed to the other world. This is illustrated in the tapestry known as *Colonnes Jumelees*, which is sometimes used in funerals.

It appears that the motif characteristics of Islamic artifacts embody powerful themas of reality construction and lifestyle. The lack of boundaries (in terms of frames around a picture as one might see in the Louvre museum in Paris) does not seem to exist for Islamic artifacts. Rather, life and reality have no artificial frame. It is an experience in which one is completely associated or totally immersed. There are no limits. Everything is intimately and intricately interwoven with no separation. Life is not caused, it happens as a total experience that is larger than can be captured in any one totality.

In many ways, the consistent repeating patterns with variant asymmetry (e.g., slight alterations in sequencing forms) indicate endless ongoing life formativeness (e.g., DNA molecules). The Islamic culture has components of surrealistic, almost dreamlike qualities. Dreams are subjective, boundless, and imaginatively formative in a highly organic fashion. Interestingly, Muhammad was in a dream when the angel Gabriel came to him to reveal Allah and the Koran.

The lifestyle in the Islamic community seems to exemplify the motif characteristics of high-density, tightly packed, repeating sequences of patterns. Observing people of Islamic descent studying in the library of the Arab Museum, they are all sitting closely together with chairs no more than six inches apart reading various editions of newspapers. The structure of families in Islamic countries is intricately and tightly engaged. The family tree comes first, as the individual is only a branch or vine that follows the unfolding sequencing of the larger organic whole. There is no separation from the whole. There is no objectivity. There is no beginning or end and there is no cause and effect. This is the organic, infinitely repeating sequencing of subjective interfacing commonly known as dream.

The motif of Islamic culture therefore can be grasped if Westerners realize that the highly subjective and fluid intricacy of cultural life has dreamlike qualities. This does not mean such a state is not real. To Islamic culture, it is the West that is living in the illusion of secular dreaming and objectivity. To the East, Allah's light is revealed in the superimposed patterning that is their portal to the next world. The danger to this, of course, is when extremists like Mohammed Atta dreamed that smashing planes into U.S. buildings was his portal. There is a difference between the Jungian states of dreaming, mandalas, tapestries, and the collective unconscious and the delusionary distortion of an entranced terrorist.

NIGHT AND DAY: YOU ARE THE "ONE"

While it may appear that the cultural motifs of East and West are as different as night and day, it is important to remember that night and day are only facets of one 24-hour cycle. Both are necessary to complete the whole and both interface continually. There are elements of surrealism in American art forms. In fact, many Americans are highly attracted to surrealistic art (e.g., Salvador Dali). The West constantly seeks altered states of consciousness (e.g., alcoholism, drug abuse, gambling, roller coasters, and television). The East also has elements of the West beginning to challenge the constraints of its religion on scientific education (Bloom, 1995).

Perhaps if we learn enough about each other's "sleeping habits" (e.g., when to leave sleeping dogs lie and when to rise to the occasion of change and innovation), the East and West can learn to find the right time and place for each other's motifs. The final chapter will deal with the transformation process that is possible through accessing and mastering one another's unique cultural motif and the dialogues that they can permit.

Chapter 10

THE EVOLUTION OF GLOBAL MOTIFS

Transformation can be understood in terms of experiences that evolve into innovative, synergistic life-forms (e.g., interfacing cultural motifs). They are dialectical. Dialectical implies two or more entities in some way distinctively defined by a boundary (such as a shape or form) able to influence one another's formativeness. This can occur within or between various levels of organization including part-whole boundary interactions. Examples are the nucleus of a human nerve defined by its own membrane distinguishing it from the rest of the cell body. The nucleus and cell body mutually interact and define one another in transforming ways.

In similar fashion, the individual is a formative, evolving process influenced by both internal (e.g., psychophysiological) activity mutually defining and interacting with external (e.g., psycho-social-cultural) environments. The dialectical interactivity of one's personal, inner voice conversing with external audible voices of the psycho-social-cultural world generates formative transformations. Such dialectical exchanges can also occur at the state-country level and at the country-global level. The hierarchy of global organization necessitates dialectical exchange to fashion formativeness. These dialectical exchanges or conversations result from a clearly defined boundary or membrane that is sufficiently permeable to permit an interactive flow.

THE SOUNDS OF SILENCE

Sculptors can create statues that are so realistic in shape, form, contour, and detail that they actually appear to be alive as if they were about to say or do something. One only needs to be patient and attentive to hear the "sounds of the statue's voice" in the pending silence. This suspended pause allows the richness of the artwork's moment to truly speak to you as if in a dialogue. All great art is actually an art-iculation of a living experience distinguished or delineated by some shape or form. It is this unique shape or design form that gives any particular work of art its membrane or motif, if you will.

MAPPING MOTIFS AND SELECTIVE MEMBRANES

Upon reviewing any world map, one can identify or articulate where the North American, Asian, and European continents are simply by the shapes and contours present. The same can be done for countries and regions of cultural influence (e.g., which countries are Islamic, which speak French or English, etc.).

The point is that cultural motifs exist and propagate in similar fashion as cells of the human body, human beings, or states within a country. There must be healthy, formative membranes (or borders) that are both distinctive, yet permeable. That means what is healthy for cells, people, and states is also healthy for cultural motifs. This should come as no surprise because no matter what level of organization one operates on, formativeness is the essential quality for all life transformation.

The unique formative nature of cultural motifs requires healthy, permeable boundaries to transform because that is their nature. As boundary conditions become more refined and permeable, they are more capable of filtering in or out what can enhance healthy transformations. The human body is constantly assimilating what it needs for growth and eliminating its waste. Individuals and states do this regarding jobs, relationships, and goal adjustment to more accurately relate to ongoing, here-and-now needs and growth concerns. Boundaries act as a selective membrane importing valuable resources (be it vitamins, healthy people, or oil, depending on the level we are on). They can also filter out invading viruses, terrorists, and excess foreign imports.

Cultural motifs engage in similar processes (e.g., immigration laws, import-export tariffs, or slanted news media). These filtering devices are critical. Each cultural motif must evolve its own rate of change and growth in a way that matches and resonates with that culture's own nature. If the rate of change is too rapid, extinction can occur (e.g., asteroids altering Earth's environment faster than the dinosaurs could possibly adapt). If there is no pressure to change or evolve, stagnation and maladaption (e.g., overpopulation and loss of food supply and developmental delays) could also adversely affect a culture. This is what happened to the Islamic world when Europe shifted its marketing trade routes to the New World of the west (Leonard, 2002). Exchange narrowed to a trickle and the Islamic culture ceased to grow and transform. Its isolation and rigid, religious fusion contributed to the stagnation of its cultural motif. That is why it is so unprepared to deal with the explosive changes of postmodernism. Postmodernism may be to the Islamic motif an invasive form of terrorism.

GLOBALIZATION AND GORILLAS

The present trend toward globalization has not attended to the nurturance, protection, and respect of the differential growth rates in the vast mosaic of cultural motifs. The large and powerful cultural motifs (e.g., the United States, and the European community) are like gorillas overpowering and flooding the third world and other smaller, less developed countries with advanced technology and intense pop-culture exportation. This was previously presented concerning how globalization has increased the exposure of countries and cultures to one another's influence and, at times, intimidation. The present increase on world terrorism appears to correspond to increasing globalization. It is not clear if there is a causal relationship involved, but the appearance of a correlation seems possible. In addition, the present intense focus on using military means to solve threats to world peace (e.g., incessant focus on war with Iraq) seems to overshadow more fundamental needs to examine our foreign policy and the effects of globalization on the vast mosaic of cultural motifs.

THE PUSH OF BUSH

As of the time of this writing, President George W. Bush has made a continual push for military action against Iraq, seeking a regime change. Protecting America is a top priority that no one in his or her right mind would even question. How and what to do to achieve this are the real questions. The evidence for Saddam Hussein having, or potentially having, weapons of nuclear mass destruction continues to be inconclusive. What is conclusive is the incessant, repetitive push by Bush to stress war as the only real alternative to settling the issue. Even as the United Nations inspectors are in Iraq, President Bush appeared to be anticipating war (with a growing military buildup in the region).

The focus here is not to establish a critique of our president. Rather, it is to highlight how American foreign policy is primarily reactive in times of stress and urgency. After September 11, the United States had tremendous international support. However, our aggressive, Monday-morning-quarterback policy demonstrates a bipolar response of either slacking off in intelligence use for pre-emptive action or paranoid, overreaction. Such swings in coping strategy suggest that both America's boundaries and those of other countries with which we deal are in jeopardy of being unbalanced and inappropriately permeable.

U.S. immigration policy literally reflects such polarities. Before September 11, the United States actually lost contact with and did not pursue immigrants coming into the United States. After September 11, it is almost impossible to acquire a green card even by the most legitimate foreign scientists. While the latter is understandable in light of recent events, it's almost like closing the barn door after the horses have all run off. Timing is everything. Terrorist sleeper cells continue to operate in the United States long after the borders have been closed.

EVILDOERS: THE ROOTS OF ALL EVIL

The horror of 9/11 rings with echoing resonance throughout America (and the world, to a lesser extent). President Bush referred to those responsible (e.g., bin Laden and his gang of Al Qaeda thugs) as the evildoers. Certainly evil was involved in the 9/11 attacks. It is never going to be eradicated without getting to the roots of all evil such as this. It is not money, but poor maintenance of boundary integrity involving cultural motifs that is at the heart or root of evil such as 9/11. The people of Islamic countries (not the governments) are the embodiment of a culture's motif. It is to the citizens that permeable boundaries nurturing cultural motifs need to be addressed. After all, terrorism emerges from extremist derivatives of the populace, not from the government per se. As a consequence, it is the populace that needs to be cultivated, nurtured, and respected. The U.S. ambassador to Saudi Arabia has indicated that the general Saudi population is conservative, ritualistic, and nondemocratic. It is from this pool of human populace that most of the 9/11 terrorists emerged. Yet, America has no clear diplomacy to deal with this fundamental cultural time bomb.

While the United States has worked through negotiations with Islamic governments involving U.S. military troops and bases, it has not considered the dire impact that the perception of a Western power's presence on Islamic soil has on the populace. Whatever the military needs and strategies may have been, the indifference to what is known as the Arab street can be profoundly disturbing.

Further confounding such perceptions is America's continued support of Israel. While clearly a critical issue in American foreign policy, efforts need to be made by the West to demonstrate cultural support for Islamic boundaries. There has been remarkable inconsistency in this as the United States has demonstrated support for totalitarian regimes of Islamic countries, which has little or no effect on the populace. It has contributed toward division in Islamic countries (e.g., Saudi Arabia), encouraging class structures of elitist and the lower echelons.

There is irony regarding the evildoers in that the roots of evil lie in their rootlessness of alienation and separatism from their own core cultural motifs. Stagnant motifs, as in Saudi populace, are toxic breeding grounds in which radicalizations can mutate. After all, a cancer is an aberrant mutation with a core structural design alien to its host (e.g., rootlessness). If cancers can be successfully treated (in many cases) through restricting the blood flow that nurtures them, then terrorism can at least be reduced, if not eliminated, through redirecting social, financial, and cultural resources toward supplanting cultural roots. Vast sums of financial and psychosocial moral support flow into terrorist groups such as Al Qaeda. This is a consequence of an impoverished populace starving for nourishment of its own psychosocial cultural identity. Redirecting the lifeblood of a country's time, energy, and resources can transform its underdeveloped culture into mature motifs. Such redirection simultaneously restricts the resource flow into cancerous infrastructures of terrorist groups.

CONTEXTUAL TRANSFORMATIONS

The transformation of cultural motifs (e.g., Saudi Arabia, Iran, Palestine, and Israel) involves creating healthy, contextual settings. In a healthy context, definitive, permeable boundaries are possible. Cultural motifs can evolve through healthy dialogues across these boundaries that emerge both within cultural motifs and between them. For example, Saudi Arabia, with the enormous wealth of its oil-rich family, lacks definitive, permeable boundaries within its own cultural motif. There needs to be internal, cultural differentiation of its populace (e.g., women's freedom, greater self-expression, religious moderation, etc.). This does not mean it needs to become an Americanized democracy. It does mean its unique cultural motifs need to be attended to in ways that pace and nurture the growth of its social, political, and religious characteristics.

We in the West tend to think that there are only two realities: (1) Americanized democracy to spread throughout the world and (2) tainted or totalitarian regimes to eliminate and convert to our way of life. The third dimension is the way of the cultural motif. As each motif has its own unique, artistic formativeness, attending and nurturing the unique, characteristic signatures of what are core features of a culture's motif set in motion powerful processes for transformative evolution. These processes include definitive, permeable boundaries, dialectical interactivity between these boundaries, and the self-propagation of a healthy context for ever-greater growth in the future

The cultural motif is like any motif. It is a unique, unfolding set of core characteristics that can never be completely categorized or stereotyped. It is a family of processes and unfolding characteristics where no one character embodies the whole. In any family, no individual member (e.g., mother, father, son, daughter, cat, dog, fish, rodent, etc.) can ever totally be or represent the whole family. Rather, there is artistry as to how the range or sets of family characteristics unfold in a mosaic, multifaceted in nature. Yet, there are identifiable themes that permeate the family's mosaic (witness the Kennedy family's or the Bushes'). The dimensions of a self-organizing entity such as a family system are similar to fractals, polymers, DNA molecules, and the universe. In other words, they are self-organizing entities with their own unique set of unfolding characteristics. They defy pigeonholing (this leads to cultural stereotyping and misunderstanding), yet are imbued with interspersed themes that convey their own unique signature.

The French have a phrase for this kind of experience: je ne sais quoi. Loosely translated, it refers to that unique, indefinable set of qualities a person or motif has that is special. It's like saying a person has that something—"I do not know what." It implies that the unique set of qualities is beyond words. In a sense, that is what cultural motifs imply. There is something distinctive and special about them. Yet, their core essences are beyond simple words. That is the unique artistry of each culture's motif. It is to such unique, artistic signature motifs that cultures need to nurture and create as a healthy context for transformative growth.

The context and the transformative evolution of maturing motifs in cultures are not separate, cause-effect reactions. Rather, they are synergistic. Transformation involves a change in a person's values, priorities, and core self. It involves a shift in the context of choices from which to draw (e.g., not just being better in a job or reshaping one's thinking or problem-solving strategies, but shifting the very context of choices). This shift in contextual choices can mean attending to the fundamental reality and assumptions from which that person or culture operates. It can mean challenging values, altering assumptions that have supported lifelong careers, and engaging in dialogues of which cultural facets best suit an individual or population at any given time and place.

There are cyclic interactions of boundaries, dialectics, and healthy contexts that allow for motif transformation. The very act of engaging in these processes is the cultural motif in action. It is both caused and affected by itself at each level of operation. In other words, the means whereby cultural motifs transform into artistic configurations is as much a part of the way motifs function as is their product. A culture's motif develops and unfolds in ways that are characteristic of the motif itself. The Saudi populace can maintain its conservative themes growing, slowing, and moving stepwise into newer variations of self-expression and role differentiation.

The present climate of globalization does not foster an ecologically healthy transformative context. The necessary attention fostering definitive, permeable boundaries that encourage interactive dialogue in nurturing contexts is not forthcoming. Where is the foreign policy from the West or the East that prioritizes and values each culture's unique motifs? The emphasis on war, conflict, and political positioning flies in the face of the aforementioned dynamics.

It is not just the United States that seems to have a reactive approach to world issues. France, Russia, North Korea, Asia, South Africa, the Ivory Coast are all examples of countries that have their own political interests. For example, Russia resists attacking Iraq because Iraq owes Russia billions of dollars of debt. France also does business with Iraq and could lose money in a war. North Korea plays the nuclear weapons program development power card to blackmail the United States (extortion is another word for it) into paying it off in vast sums of money. Then it proceeds to develop nuclear weapons anyway.

The international environment is a mosaic of quid pro quo, dialectical arrangements, and designs constantly in a state of flux and metamorphosis. China is part of the United Nations Security Council, which the United States needs both for its supporting vote on Iraq and to assist (along with Japan's prime minister) in peacefully pressuring North Korea to disassemble its nuclear weapons program.

In all this wheeling and dealing (countries paying off one another in international negotiations has been called the price of doing business), there needs to be a voice and spirit initiated regarding the nurturing of a healthy context for transforming cultural motifs. The international scene is already an expression of this motif mosaic. It would only take a transformation of consciousness to recognize such global design structures as representing substantial roots expressing the cultural motifs of each country. At least that would transform the ground of dialogue into a new context that re-envisions a new form of globalization.

TRANSFORMATION THROUGH CONTEXTUAL GLOBALIZATION

Transformation invokes new levels (e.g., the context of cultures) of choice (Naim, 2002). For example, living in one culture (e.g., America) suggests a set of values and rules of perceiving reality in a core way. The constructs of doing and achieving are highly valued in America. Therefore, the range of choices is defined and constrained by the context of the culture. Discovering that doing and achieving are not the only constructs in which one may make choices is transforming in itself. To effect a change in the person means to alter the fundamental values and constructs of that person's reality.

Cultures need to act on the international context in which their motifs are embedded (Stiglitz, 2002). The international mosaic of quid pro quo arrangements contextually defines and constrains the choices and manifestations of cultural motifs. Challenging these ongoing contractual negotiations encourages transformation at global levels. America's need for support from Russia for the Iraq War causes it to be reticent in its criticism of human rights violations. Saudi Arabia's need for U.S. military hardware causes it to walk a thin line between allowing America full access of its airports and alienating its Muslim population. The oil-producing countries are favored with superficial acknowledgment and patronizing gestures. Yet, nowhere is there genuine value and respect for one another's cultural motifs. The criteria seem to be "a friend in need is a friend in deed." Such a global, contextual quid pro quo will never engender global stability and harmony.

Creating a contextual transformation means recognizing a country's cultural motif as an entity with a unique consciousness. Recognition that all countries have a unique consciousness in their cultural motifs transforms the global context into a mosaic of interfacing motifs. Such an interface of mosaic motifs is not static but dynamically interactive in dialectical activity.

The transformative capacities of interactive, cultural motifs within and between countries are represented in quid pro quo arrangements. Transformative capacities can be embedded in unhealthy adaptations. When the United States has to tone down its criticism of Russia for human rights violations instead of honest confrontations, it conveys messages that are manipulative and insincere. While politics may require compromise, statesmanship requires integrity. If America and Russia truly want to be allies, they, like all good friends who respect one another's uniqueness and integrity, can endure honest confrontations. The short- and long-term gains come into play at this point. If America is to convey and receive respect as a member of the global community, it must adhere to a high standard of integrity. If we lose an ally because we are true in adhering to our own values, what have we really lost? We tried to buy off North Korea with financial aid to prevent their development of nuclear weapons. They took our money and went ahead and developed them anyway. Raising the bar of recognition demonstrating genuine value for Russia's cultural motif (as well as for that of all countries) creates a new context for global transformation. When countries and their cultural motifs remain true to themselves, real diplomacy and transformation are possible.

In a similar fashion, America's genuine recognition of Islamic cultural motifs would go far toward establishing genuine, mutual respect. The question is asked sometimes by Americans, "Why are we hated in the East?" It appears that Americans have no ill will toward Islamic countries, and it seems incomprehensible why they should have animosity toward us. Yet, time and again, it is demonstrated that America has no real concept of how it misunderstands and, as perceived by Muslim countries, violates sacred, cultural motifs. It is not only about U.S. military presence in Muslim territory and the Israeli-Palestinian conflict, it is about cultural intimidation. The critical nature of such intimidation is the fused admixture of sacred ritual intertwined with psycho-social-cultural tradition. Motifs involve an inseparable synergy of these multilevel dimensions infused into a dynamic, wholistic cultural identity. When scientific advancements are introduced in single-minded ways which ignore the motifs cultural complexity, perceptions of transgression can be provoked. The motif of change for the West is rapid. For the East, change must be anchored to the already existing Islamic history of their universe. The complexities are subtle. The devil is in the details of idiosyncratic motifs.

America has much more advanced cultural motifs in terms of technological and postmodern achievements. Yet, it is a young country lacking in historical values and tradition (in comparison with Eurasian and Eastern cultures). While it is less driven by its historical roots, allowing greater facility of futuristic change, it lacks the empathy and comprehension of the powerful impact such advancements have on the subtle differences in cultural motifs.

The pragmatic motif of America scoffs at the subtle difference in culture and language. For example, referring to a tomato as "tomato" or "tomahto" makes no difference when ordering in an American restaurant. However, the subtle use of "tomahto" conveys a message about what and how that person thinks and functions. There is a consciousness to that nuanced accent. The reference to soft drinks as "soda" or "pop" is another subtle difference that can make a difference depending on if you were raised on the coast or the Midwest. There are endless regional differences in America alone that identify northerners from southerners, east coast from west coast. It's almost a standard that people in Chicago are always working and people in California think Chicagoans are strange for doing so. Of course, Chicagoans have their own opinion of California lifestyle as well. The cultural variations between countries are even more powerfully defining. An American (from any region) stands out in European and Islamic countries like a firecracker at midnight. The subtle differences are so powerful between interacting cultural motifs as to create frustrations at best and intense conflicts at worse. Witness an American ordering dinner in Paris who is fatigued, speaks no French, and upset that his waiter keeps bringing him the wrong order. Sometimes it's comical, sometimes it's tragic.

Language and sounds create powerful states of consciousness (Feeney, 1999). If 93 percent of all communication is nonverbal, the unique, phonetic sounds of each cultural motif's language exert powerful effects on meaning and reality. For example, Americans speaking Arabic may not capture the precise phoneme sounds of Arabic characters. As a consequence, inaccurate meaning and messages are communicated. Language and meaning are intimately tied together (Chomsky, 1967). It is very difficult when raised in one culture to pronounce sounds of another's. The cultural motif's uniqueness is manifest in such circumstances.

Transforming cultural motifs on a global level requires a recognition and respect for their interactive dialogue. When members of the United Nations are communicating in different languages requiring translation, great skill is required to capture the essence and meaning. Translating the essence of meaning from one language phoneme to another in the vernacular of that language is a daunting task.

Recognition and realization of the unique, subtle differences existing among cultural motifs set up transforming dialogues between them. For example, how do the American English letters *o* and *r* differ from the

French or Spanish? Interestingly enough, there are no *o*s and *r*s in Arabic. Now what do we do? How do we communicate? How do we have a dialogue without a common language? Is it like the Tower of Babel, where no one can understand another, as we are all so different? Our differences cannot be glossed over in some overgeneralized, cookie-cutter way. The smaller our worlds become, the more glaring and significant are these subtle differences in motifs. That similar phenomena of reality may be construed in many different ways can be evidenced on a variety of dimensions. For example, a person from America may make a negative assertion, saying "no" to a request by a friend. A person raised in an Arabic culture would interpret a single negative assertion as a "yes" (Sue & Sue, 1990). The distinction is what is known as high context versus low context. High-context conditions are anchored in the physical situation or internalized within the person. The Arabic culture is high context. Therefore, an American would have to excessively (by Western standards) stress the negative assertion "no" numerous times when having a dialogue in Arabic settings. It is an understatement to suggest that an Arabic person won't take no for an answer. It takes many nos. It is a mistake to assume that power is the only thing the Arabic culture understands as Charles Krauthammer (2001) has suggested. It is more about context of communication than power in itself.

The low-context conditions typical of cultures of the West (e.g., America) relies more on the verbal part of the message than the contextual stressing that is nonverbal. Low context is associated with more optimism and individualization. High-context cultures operate in more group-oriented societies emphasizing rules of law and procedure (Sue & Sue, 1990).

The United States is also low context when compared with Switzerland, Germany, and Scandinavia. Asians, Hispanics, blacks, Native Americans as well as other minority groups in America are all high-context cultures. The advantage of high context is that because the meaning of language expressions and events are so highly articulated and defined, communication is faster, more economical, efficient, and satisfying (Sue & Sue, 1990). Because high context is more embedded in cultural mores and motifs, it is slow to change, cohesive, and unifying. It's almost as if there is a language about the spoken language (e.g., metalinguistic) that cultural insiders already know.

Low context is not unifying but can change rapidly and easily. Observe the ever-changing slang, colloquialisms, and wordplay innovations constantly evolving in America and other low-context Western countries.

These qualities of cultural motif are well suited for high-powered, post-modern societies of the West. These differentials in language patterns and linguistics between the West and East can create difficulty in dialogue if left unrecognized.

They also reflect the cultural motifs of the West (fast changing, future oriented, individual-freedom seeking) and the East (maintaining historical ritual, anchoring to the origins, and slow to change group cohesiveness). Recognizing global contextualization of cultural motifs (e.g., mosaic of interactive cultural motifs) is critical in comprehending the unique diversity of cultural linguistics.

The structure and design of language is directly related to the reality, meaning, and formativeness of each culture's unique motif. Respect and experiential learning in the mosaic of multicultural motifs facilitates dialogue and global transformation.

PARALANGUAGE IN CULTURAL MOTIFS

There are other dimensions to linguistic structure and design. These include loudness, pauses, silences, hesitations, rate of speech, and inflection. Cultures vary along these and other dimensions depending on the nature and design of their unique motifs. There are variations in how to greet as well as taking turns in who talks and who listens (Mehrabian, 1972; Mehrabian & Ferris, 1976). Cultural motifs also vary in rule complexity regarding when to speak and to yield (Dublin, 1973; Jansen, 1985).

Americans are relatively uncomfortable with pauses and stretched silences, feeling pressure and obligations to talk or say something to fill in the breaks. Other cultures structure and design silences in a wide variety of ways according to their cultural motifs. The English and Arabs use silences as a form of privacy. Russians, the French, and Hispanics interpret pauses as a sign of agreement in social occasions. Asians use silence as a symbol of respect for their elders. The Chinese and Japanese structure the meaning of silence in their political encounters as a desire to continue speaking after making a point. Silence is a symbol of continuing, not ending.

The many diverse ways of structuring meaningful, linguistic designs in each culture's motif are readily apparent. Dialectical interactivity can occur if there is a contextualization recognizing how multicultural motifs reconfigure reality and meaning. Participating cultures need to be willing to suspend egocentric, the-world-revolves-around-me motif thinking to enter into these new worlds of reality and meaningful exchange. Perhaps one source of aggravation toward developing an awareness of global context is having one language (e.g., English) be viewed as the language of the world. Language structures our constructs of reality and religion at all levels. Even the concept of God is framed as "this is the 'word' of God." Yet, a rose by any other name (or language) conveys different meanings of reality. The pen is indeed mightier than the sword. With English as the predominant world language, the global effects on the mosaic of multicultural motifs cannot be underestimated. Now more than ever cultural uniqueness needs to be advocated.

In America, children are raised to be expressive and free-spirited. Foreigners observe and misconstrue (because of their mental sets of embedded motifs) such behavior as brash, immodest, rude, and disrespectful (Jansen, 1985). Teachers embedded with American motifs misperceive minority children who are silent as reticent to speak because they are ignorant, lack motivation and so on. Such teachers fail to accurately interpret minority children's silent behavior as an attempt to demonstrate respect for their elders. Unfortunate and unnecessary conflicts and frustrations can ensue if multicultural motifs are not provided a contextualized setting for dialogue.

Other paralanguage dimensions involve volume, intensity, and proxemics (closeness). Americans are raised in a cultural motif that encourages extraversion. Adults behaving in loud and exuberant ways, like children, are misinterpreted by foreigners as boisterous and shameless. Asians tend to be introverted and soft spoken and misinterpret Americans' loudness as aggression, anger, and signs of loss of control. The possible perception of threat and hostility on their part can be unnecessarily elevated.

Compared to Arabs, Americans are soft spoken (Sue & Sue, 1990). Arabs enjoy being bathed in sound. They may turn up the volume of radios, televisions, and recorders. One reason for this is that by keeping the volume loud, their neighbors who cannot afford these luxuries can also hear and enjoy them (Sue & Sue, 1990). However, in America where practically everyone has these, it's considered rude and an invasion of privacy to play them at high volumes. Like beauty, appropriateness is beheld in the eye of the motif.

Proximities that deal with how close or far to be with one another also are a function of motifs. The perception and use of interpersonal space (Hall, 1966) involves four zones in America. These are (1) intimacy has a range of 18 inches, (2) personal space has a range of one and one-half to four feet, (3) socializing has a range of 4 to 12 feet, and (4) public domain has a range of greater than 12 feet.

As with other dimensions, appropriate ranges vary with the culture's motif involved. Arabs, Africans, blacks, and the French enjoy closer spaces for interpersonal conversations than Anglo-Saxon cultures. Positioning oneself at any particular range of closeness may be construed as an act of impoliteness or sign of deep respect and intimacy.

There are also cultural differences in how affirmations or criticisms are expressed and manifested in accord to operant motifs. For example, the Asian expression of criticism (Sue & Sue, 1990) occurs not in words but in contextual factors. These factors involve the (1) amount of time used to praise, (2) amount of time spent to derogate oneself, (3) descriptions used, and (4) types of questions asked.

An example of the preceding occurred at an Asian science conference. After the presentation of a research paper, a member of the audience rose to inquire regarding its merits. He stated that he had only two questions. These were (1) How did the researcher decide to use this particular research methodology and (2) How did he select the particular population to be researched? The context of asking these questions indicated that (1) the wrong methodology was employed and (2) the researcher's defined population was deficient in representing the whole (Sue & Sue, 1990). The criticism was in asking the questions in the way they were asked, not in the researcher's response.

Contextual factors such as these are driven and determined by the culture's motif. Only by using contextualization of cultural motifs can meaning and synergistic dialogues transpire and transform multiple motifs.

HARMONIZING THE MUSIC OF MOTIFS

It is in the recognition of motifs that exist in all cultural formats that this common ground can be established. The artistry and unique subtleties of each allows for a dialectical of comparisons and contrasts. Without recognition of a culture's artistry, there can be no dialectical interaction or transformation. This is where the powerful forces of synergy converge. Formativeness becomes the foundation upon which all cultural motifs are grounded. This then becomes the global context for which genuine transformation of world harmony can begin to emerge.

The dialectical between motifs many times consists of a cacophony of sights, sounds, and senses. The speed and tempo with which people of different cultural motifs speak, move, and visualize can be seen as the musical chaos of a symphonic orchestra tuning itself. Each musician tunes his or her instrument prior to coming into harmonizing resonance as a whole.

Notice that the holism of a symphony orchestra is not that all instruments and sections are playing identical notes at the same time. Rather, contextual holism is the resonant flow of harmonizing sequence and syntax of one musical movement orchestrated (i.e., formatively arranged and coherently organized) relative to another.

The sequencing and syntax are experiential as well as conceptual of a formative musical reality and consciousness. In order to grasp and understand the sights, sounds, and visual world of musical orchestration, the full range of sensory experience is essential.

Dialectical interaction within and between cultural motifs also requires the full range of sensory and conceptual experience to bring order and meaning to otherwise incoherent sensations. Listening to people speak various foreign languages completely unknown to the listener is an experience of chaos and confusion. The uneducated and inexperienced listener has no way of making order and meaning of the spoken sounds of the foreign language. It can leave the listener in a confused, curious, and disoriented state. Without connection of the sound, word concept, and sensory experience, sophisticated language motifs are simply noise and distraction.

It is not unlike the Helen Keller experience of learning. Only when her teacher, Ann Sullivan, engaged her with the experiential interface of the word sound "water" (actually it was with the mouth movement as Helen was deaf and speechless) and running water itself, did Keller grasp the meaning of the noise (movement). There were elements of Helen Keller's experience as a child where the experience of water was familiar. Discovering common elements that may exist between cultural motifs can bridge gaps of experiential communication.

Dialectical motifs need such experiential interfacing to truly discern meaning and order out of noise. The dialectical of interactive motifs involves stretching oneself (or one's cultural motif) to experientially translate one set of learned experiences into the motif of another's culture. Such a stretch may mean letting go of one frame of reference to reorganize into the other.

WAR OF FORMATIVENESS

How does one think in French? Such a question suggests that to speak a language, dialogue within and between motifs, one needs to alter one's internal cognition and schematic design. To step into and out of cultural motifs, learning how to transform from one design configuration to another is critical. It is beyond pure cognition. Transforming is a total mind-body immersion. Total immersion into a language is considered a highly effective way of learning it. The same is true for how to access the transformativeness from one cultural motif to another. Immersion into an empathic, mind-body alteration of formativeness allows for an interactive dialogue of motifs. Involved in such alterations is the ability to shift shape and design of one's mind-body configuration to think, feel, and act in that new identity of motif. For example, when an Anglo-American wants to express an emotion, the linguistic structure is one of personal identification. The statement "I am crazy about this girl" is a case in point. A French person uses a different linguistic. The expression involves saying something like "I have 'bad' foolishness for her." French linguistics involve a design structure of possessing a condition, not being a condition (that is, identification). French also uses more interactive word patterns (e.g., "bad" foolishness, where "bad" is not equivalent to the English "bad" of wrong or evil).

The linguistics of a language (e.g., structure of syntax, phonetics, stress, and marking patterns) reflects a culture's motif. Understanding distinctive differences assists in comprehending sensory and symbolic meaning of these motifs. Thinking in French means speaking phonetically in that language. The sensory sound, flow, and patterning of spoken language create the unique, meaningful experience of that cultural motif.

Rhythm and intonation are powerful, nonverbal components of a culture's spoken language. For example, spoken English has individual word syllables given varying degrees of stress. Notice how the words "librarian" and "library" are pronounced with the syllables receiving varying degrees of stress. The French words "bibliothecaire" and "bibliotheque" are spoken with each syllable receiving the same stress level.

As a result of differential stress patterns, the speech rhythms in both languages are altered (Smith & LeZotte, 2002). Alterations in rhythms, syntax, and pace affect meaning and reality (Feeney, 1999; Chomsky, 1967). Consider the pronunciation of the following English sentences:

1. Sue lives here (three syllables; three primary stresses).
2. Susie enjoys music (six syllables, only three primary stresses on syllables one, three, and five).

Spoken English uses primary stresses known as stress-timed speech (Smith & LeZotte, 2002). French rhythm is markedly different:

1. Elles arrivent (three syllables, all equal stress).
2. Elles arrivent à six heures (six syllables, all with equal stress).

Speaking French is contingent on the number of syllables present. Such a pattern is known as syllable-timed speech (Smith & LeZotte, 2002). Because the second French sentence has twice as many syllables (six), it will take twice as much time to pronounce as compared to the first.

Intonation patterns also vary in French and English. The pitch rises at the end of each phrase within a French sentence, falling on the last syllable of the sentence. It may rise higher on the last syllable when asking a question (Smith & LeZotte, 2002).

What is intriguing about these linguistic patterns (motifs) is how their expression in English and French correlates to cultural motifs. There are clear pattern breaks in the way people speaking English enunciate. The digital, separate, discrete English patterning is reflected in the concrete, pragmatic, analytic cause-and-effect orientation of a problem-solving cultural motif. The fluid, holistic, rhythmic flow of continuous French phonetic pronunciation reflects the poetic merger of moment-to-moment flow.

The sensory experience of rhythm and intonation can alter meaning, quality of personal experience, and symbolism and states of consciousness (Csikszentmihalyi, 1990). Linguistic experts (Mocuta, 2001) have suggested that there is something unique to each language pattern that is untranslatable. It is je ne sais quoi—"it's something, I do not know what!" It is this untranslatable uniqueness that lies at the core of every language's linguistic patterning, which reflects that culture's unique motif. It is at the very heart and soul of that culture's consciousness (Mocuta, 2001). This is the reflective spirituality of that culture's unique motif (Feeney, 2001).

Arriving at the culture's soul of unique motif requires knowing in a very special way. It requires attention, patience, and deep respect. The ancient philosopher Ovid expressed that to know is to love (connaître c'est aimer). The unique variances in how English and French words are expressed illustrate how to know and value their motifs. The word "know" is construed differently (as one would expect) in English and in French. In English, the word "know" has multiple meanings (for example, knowledge, experience, and familiarity). This is consistent with its linguistic motif of stressed-time speech and digital thinking. The French version of "knowing" (e.g., connaître) implies being reborn. When two people connaître one another, they are coming into the world of that experience in a new way of knowing one another as if they are being reborn together (e.g., marriage, deep love, etc.). This is consistent with its syllable-timed speech, sense of continuity, and analogue thinking. What happens if you place a digital thinker with one who is analogue? That contrast is reflected in many of the controversies arising between American and French politics. English tends to be spoken as prose. French tends to be spoken in rhythms similar to poetry. Not surprisingly, the concept of reality is slightly different for the French and the Americans. In English, one expresses negation as "I do not have..." (e.g., "I do not have a book"). The negation simply refers to not having or possessing the physical object of a book. The French expression "Je n'ai pas d'un livre" not only says there is no physical expression of the object (e.g., "I have no book"), it also implies the image of the book is not possessed.

Such a notion is literally foreign to English-speaking cultural motifs. Yet, this is quite consistent with the French philosopher René Descartes, who poised the famous question, "If a tree falls in the forest but no one is there experience it, did it really fall?" Such philosophical questioning reflects a motif of how to construct reality. The French negation implies that the image of the object, as well as the object itself, is not possessed and therefore may not be a reality for that person. To paraphrase Ovid, to truly and deeply know a culture's unique motif is to love it (e.g., *connaître c'est aimer*).

Thinking in French, American English, or Arabic invokes different linguistic patterns, design structures, and consciousness of meaningful realities. There are, of course, many word-phrase patterns in one language that defy direct, word-for-word translation into another. Cultural motifs operate in similar fashions. One has an experience of some phenomenon of living. How one selectively filters one set of qualities of that experience over another is determined by operant, cultural motifs of that individual. One might suggest that making love in French may be experienced in a way subtly different from love American-style. It's an apple-and-orange dynamic. What might that experience be in Arabic or Chinese? Love is love but is it precisely the same equivalent the world over? Indeed, the small differences can make the real difference. After all, the genetic configuration the human being's DNA compared to that of a chimpanzee differs by barely 3 percent. One could only imagine that making love to a chimpanzee (theoretically) just might be subtly different than making love to the all-American girl next door.

Cultural motifs exert forces upon one another to shape and design others into their own image. Without embracing a transformative global context, cultural motifs can collapse into warring conflicts of either/or formativeness. Instead of learning how to dialogue interactively, cultural motifs reify into warring efforts of one rigid motif trying to absorb or usurp that of another. Military wars, where one country exerts physical force to alter another country's cultural motif, are not the only way wars of formativeness operate. There can be wars of information, media, politics, terrorism, economics, and of course, religion. While the medium and levels of intervention vary, they are all wars of formativeness. They are all ways in which one form of life attempts to change, alter, or transform the design structure of another. This is not unlike what Charles Darwin referred to as evolution of the species. Actually, evolution is about evolving forms of life. As such, evolution is formativeness in action.

Warring formativeness is not a matter of good or evil. It is just the nature of life-forms. Evil is not creating a context for all forms. Cultural motifs are living entities. They will pressure to perpetuate themselves. Whether they synergize with other motifs, absorb, or are absorbed by other cultures depends on the nature of interactivity. Transformative global contextualization can provide a format for synergizing all cultural motifs. Just as water seeks its own level, so cultural motifs seek to express and proliferate themselves one way or another.

Providing a global contextualization for cultural motifs to dialogue creates the best-case scenario allowing all cultural motifs to synergize. America is facing serious threats from terrorism spreading throughout the globe. While it has to take immediate homeland protective and military actions, these are not long-term solutions. Al Qaeda has regrouped in Indonesia, instigating continuous anti-American efforts. While America has pursued terrorism in Afghanistan and other countries, long-term results will only be discerned at the transformative level of global contextualization for all cultural motifs. Such a contextualization informs the mosaic of cultural motifs to engage in meaningful dialogue to generate synergy. It is in this synergistic dialogue that transformative motifs can emerge on a global level.

Muslim and American motifs are remarkably distinctive and unique. Building respect, experiential immersion, and recognition for their differential cultural motifs lays the groundwork for long-term solutions. As these cultural motifs are uniquely distinct at both the content and contextual levels, it is essential that there be comprehension of their unique nature.

The capacity to experience alternative cultural motifs involves the courage to align with the transformative nature of motifs themselves. Motifs are not set things (like bricks or stones). For motifs (cultural or otherwise) to sustain symmetrical and asymmetrical design structures (e.g., evolution and expansion), transformational contexts are essential. Such contextualizations imbue dimensions of open space, time, and experiential learning. There needs to be room and openness for people of diverse cultural motifs to engage in experiential learning of what's uniquely familiar and unfamiliar. Motifs need to be understood as requiring the fertile ground of open space and time to grow, evolve, and expand.

Motifs are never a finished state. Rather, they are an unfolding process of renewing formativeness. Allowing safe, nurturing, and resourceful experiential learning for the formative nature of motifs to evolve from their present state of design structure to the next moment-to-moment innovation provides fertile contexts for growth. This implies a uniquely delicate balance of movement from the status quo toward some crafted innovation.

Motifs come to life in formatively evolving new design structures that experiment with unfamiliar, unknown advancements that may or may not be creatively adaptive (e.g., what is Darwin's evolution of the species?). The risk in all cultural motifs is that they become reified into rigid, set templates where they lose the dynamic balance between homeostasis and dynamic evolution. The fall of any superpower (Roman or American) commences when the unique equilibrium of a cultural motif's stasis and dynamic formativeness is lost.

Cultural motifs require both stable roots and dynamic evolution. Symmetry and asymmetrical formativeness (East or West) are in unique equilibrium for each cultural motif. Some motifs emphasize roots (East) and others wing (West). Respect and care for both are required to balance such dynamic equilibrium.

The dangers of threat, invasion, and economic and cultural overwhelming jeopardize dynamic equilibrium with or between cultural motifs. If a culture (as with an individual) perceives itself as backed into a corner, it can risk of losing the formative capacity of dynamic equilibrium. While such experiences can challenge motifs into action, it can also stimulate overreaction (e.g., East and West jihads). All motifs are dynamic and unfinished. Yet, all function and operate in unique, asymmetrical configurations. America runs on a fast track. The East (Islamic cultures) moves in the passenger lane (with explosive movements of terrorism). No cultural motif is complete, finished, and right. Encouraging global contextualization cognizant of differential cultural motifs is critical for transformation.

SURGES IN FORMATIVENESS

There is a new surge of formativeness in America as a response to terrorism threats, for example, the reorganization of the Central Intelligence Agency and the Federal Bureau of Investigation, the establishment of the

Department of Homeland Security, the appointment of a new head of operations at the National Security Council, and the addition of over eleven hundred staff analysts at the counterterrorism center as well as covert operations, Web sites, new computer hardware, and increased cooperation with foreign intelligence and law enforcement agencies (Elliott, 2002).

Fighting terrorism, creating a global community of peace, and transforming cultural motifs toward quantum elevations invokes multifaceted dimensions. America's proactive attack on Al Qaeda in Afghanistan and dealing with President Bush's axis of evil invokes military and nonmilitary interventions (e.g., confiscating terrorists' bank accounts, shutting down phony charities that fund Al Qaeda, networking with multinational coalitions, etc.).

Responding to the terrorists' continued threats (e.g., they are regrouping and continuing attacks in Indonesia, threatening the United States with equally dangerous 9/11-like assaults) has understandably provoked increased formativeness of innovative design structures. Unfortunately, with all the bombing and advanced military and technological might of the United States, Al Qaeda, like the proverbial cockroach, continues to persevere. Could it be that we have not also struck at the roots of terrorism by creating equal formative efforts nurturing a transformative global context? We can mow down the terrorists (like dandelions in an untended lawn) endlessly. The roots of terrorism need to be destroyed not only with direct aggression but planting healthy cultural motifs throughout the gaping landscape of global topography. Dandelions always grow back if their roots are not supplanted by new, healthy seeds of grass to fill the void. Nurturing, seeding, and cultivating healthy cultural motifs in the East and West could go a long way toward undermining recurrent terrorist threats.

The war of formativeness cannot be won by direct power alone for it does not focus on the core issue of how and where to nurture healthy formativeness throughout the global community of cultural motifs. Statesmanship and diplomacy striking at core levels that encourage international formativeness throughout all cultural motifs can be transforming. A culture's motif has the inherent property of genesis (origins of life-forms) within it. By creating a globalization fostering a contextualization nurturing deep-rooted formativeness, the transformative potentials of motifs can be released.

THE ULTIMATE WAR ZONE: BATTLEGROUND FOR GOD

Israeli prime minister Sharon once expressed that the question of existence was more important than the question of peace. Cultures including those which are Christian, Jewish, and Islamic justify the primacy of their existence by aligning themselves with God. Each strives to establish the sovereign right of their existence through divine privilege. It is as though somehow one culture is more Godlike and chosen over all others.

The historical, religious figure of Abraham is a classic case in point. The great monotheistic religions of the world (e.g., Christianity, Judaism, and Islam) have all selectively distilled their own version of how Abraham is really more one religion's father than he is other two's (VanBiema, 2002). Christianity claims Abraham as its father (who is a direct link with God) in their version of Abraham's sacrifice. As Abraham was told by God to sacrifice his only son Isaac, Abraham had to have faith in God's word to attempt to carry about his command. When God intervened, Christians hailed it as a sign of God's redemption and saving grace. These qualities are embedded in Christianity.

Judaism claimed Abraham as its father for he was said to embody the covenant of faith (as manifest by Moses at the Ten Commandments). Islam claims Abraham as its father, changing the lineage of Isaac to Abraham's other son Ishmael. Characteristic of Islamic motifs, Islamics historically claim that theirs is the authorized religion as Muslim tribes trace their origins to Ishmael. Such a realignment of historical lineage with Ishmael allows Islam to lay claim as the only valid and true religion. It allows them to claim that all others are the infidels and Muslims are the only faithful in God's light.

Curiously, the existence of one religion appears to come at the expense of all others. How Godlike is that? Each religion connects with some unique aspect of God's divine mystery. Religious scholars from time immemorial promote exhortations as to the unknowable omniscience of God as divine mystery. Divine mystery precludes any one religion (or scholar) from claiming it has all-knowing, universal knowledge. Even the eminent philosopher Immanuel Kant (1998), who reached for the ultimate metaphysical reality of universal, categorical imperatives, failed to articulate actual earthbound examples. One can always speak theoretically, but God (and maybe the devil too) is in the details. There is an ancient adage with an unknown author (God, perhaps?) who suggested that no generalization was worth a damn including this one. Who will stand up and say what is moral and just at all times, all places, and in all unique configurations? Justice is blind and so is faith, which is what Abraham was being tested for in the first place.

Motifs reflect the asymmetrical, unfinished mystery of spirit and body. Cultural motifs evolve with familiar surprise. Just when one thinks one knows all of one's culture's motifs, new, innovative surprises evolve and emerge. Any religion or person fixating on fundamentalist perceptions of what God, spirit, and human beings must be would appear to violate the fundamental law of what God really is—divine mystery and all it entails.

The battle for God is not unlike the biblical story of the battle of two women over a baby each claims is her own. When the two women came before King Solomon, the wisest of all men in biblical times, he proclaimed that the child should be sliced in half with each piece being given to the women. At the moment the sword was drawn, the true mother came forth willing to release her claim to save its life. The battle over God requires similar commitment. To know God is to love God. To know that one can never fully comprehend God is to know through experience of divine mystery, God. This is a different knowing (*connaître*) and invokes being reborn. This rebirth is the child who can love God but only when the real mother releases claim to possession. Transforming cultural motifs require creating a global contextualization incarnating spirituality. Fighting over the origins of spiritual birth as in religious wars of jihad (whatever form they may take, cultural or military) shatters the growing global context of transforming cultural motifs. The rebirth of transformation can only be saved by cultures releasing sole claim of possession to God. Embracing the mosaic of cultural motifs creates global contextualization. It releases the claim of possession that the world or God belongs to any one culture. Transforming motifs acknowledge the divine mystery of a formative God.

Yes, sometimes we must fight, sometimes we must make peace, but at all times should we not strive to create a globalization that transcends the limiting values of corporate profits, national interests, and covert cultural imposition of archaic fundamentalisms? Cultural motifs need room to breathe, expand, and differentiate in safe, challenging contexts. There is no one-size-fits-all cultural motif for all other motifs. Higher-ordering principles are required for transforming cultural motifs. Is God here to serve human beings? Are human beings here to serve God? Is there an all-or-nothing bipolar resolution to such questions? Is there a universal response when encountering God as divine mystery?

What do motherhood, Abraham, and faith all have in common? Is it not in the encounter of humbling divine mystery? Globalization in any meaningful sense requires a spiritual contextualization as fertile ground for the transformational seeds of cultural motifs. The ego of undue nationalism needs to be humbled in the enlightened self-interest of global transformation.

The seeds of terrorism have wrought poisonous fruit polluting world peace and the lives of innocent people. Globalization that creates spiritual contextualization transforms the seeds of cultural motifs. Transforming cultural motifs will bring into fruition the genuine, multicultural diversity of divine mystery. The seeds of terrorism will find no place in such fertile ground nurturing the inherent spirituality of cultural motifs.

ARAB ANTI-AMERICANISM

There is the position that the roots of Arab anti-Americanism stem from political regimes in the Arab world deflecting blame to the United States for all Arab ills (Rubin, 2002). For over 50 years, the United States has clearly demonstrated pro-Arab and pro-Muslim support time and time again. This position holds that the animosity toward America is generated by self-interested factions within the Arab world. Rubin cites numerous occasions where the United States has supported pro-Arab, pro-Muslim political factions (Iraq, Egypt, and Syria when they were ruled by Soviet-friendly dictatorships). Rubin describes how the United States was wrongly accused of being an imperialist country when it exerted pressure on Cairo (e.g., when it threatened to block aid) after Egypt imprisoned a prominent human rights activist.

The problems with their position that anti-Americanism is merely a deflective blaming strategy by Arabic political groups are numerous. In the first place, Rubin (2002) addresses the issue solely on political levels of government to government. Yet, the anti-American sentiment is primarily held on the Arab street (e.g., the populace) and not always at the government level. Second, the jihads between East and West date back over a thousand years. Could such a blame game strategy have been operating in the twelfth and thirteenth centuries when England's Holy Crusades were launched against the infidel Arab world to "save the Holy Land"? Third, it has been demonstrated that no country wants the United States to support it when it means being pressured to be what the United States wants it to be (e.g., to have American democracy, American culture, etc.).

Additionally, many of the positions the United States takes are more about advocating U.S. interests than being pro- or anti-Arab. The supported Iran, Syria, and Egypt as much because of the Soviet threat as it did because of being pro-Arab. The tremendous oil-rich fields of Kuwait are critical to the energy needs of the West. Why is it that the United States is pursuing war with Iraq (it also has tremendous oil reserves) and yet exploring more peaceful diplomatic channels with nuclear-powered North Korea (which has no oil)?

These and many other aspects raise the specter of what motivates the United States. The cultural invasion by the West in the East has been a source of contention regarding women's roles, scientific research, sexual practices, divorce, music, and so on for many years. Recently, the Saudi king reflected on how reticent his people were to change their fused, social-religious, ritualized lifestyle. The Arabic populace is culturally riddled with fundamentalist ethics that prevent openness toward the outside world.

It is patently absurd to presume that the cultural intimidation by the West is not a factor in anti-American sentiments. The fact is that many of the U.S. positions have reflected not a genuine culture, but its own nationalistic efforts. When the Arab world observes the U.S. government walking a tightrope in the Middle East, it perceives America as playing both ends against the middle. The American government can be perceived as insincere, lacking deep respect for either culture. It is perceived as out for its own interests. Could it be that the reason the United States has been perceived as weak and skittish (for example, in Somalia and Lebanon) is in fact that it lacked the integrity to take a stand for what it believed was right rather than simply utilitarian?

The presumption that the Arab world only understands power may be a cultural misperception because the United States only seems to persistently take a stand when its economic, political interests are at stake, not when principles, human rights, or integrity are at issue. America goes to war against dictators that rule oil-rich countries. It deprives aid for human rights violations. There is hypocrisy in such policies, and the Arab world, like the rest of the world, may be poor but it is not deaf, dumb, or blind. When will the U.S. government learn that integrity, ethics, and genuine concern for human rights are as much worth dying for as are rogue nations that just happen to have enormous oil reserves (which, if controlled by the U.S. government, could significantly affect America's economic recovery)? Employing war games with Iraq (or equivalent Iraqlike regimes) every 10 or 11 years without exerting equally intelligent efforts to negotiate multicultural respect and integrity dehumanizes global transformation.

DEMOCRACY AND MULTICULTURALISM

The shock and horror of 9/11 challenged and provoked a renewed loyalty and patriotism in America. President Bush and his wife, Laura, enjoy one of the highest approval ratings of any presidential couple in American history. They are a kind of Ozzie and Harriet of Americana. There is a return to our historical roots of family values and down-to-earth American pragmatism. Absent are the exotica of the Clinton era. Such a return to traditional values is an understandable reaffirmation of our culture's formative motifs. When under attack (e.g., by terrorism or slumping economic times), there tends to be a nostalgic return (e.g., or regression in service of the ego) to earlier stages of development.

The dark side of such recycling into earlier times is the potential for rigidity and fundamentalist attitudes and orientations. America is remarkably diverse. Just walk into any urban coffee shop. There are literally no two people dressed alike. It's almost like an ongoing costume party where each person comes dressed in their own shtick or outfit. They are just being their wonderful, unique selves. The tolerance and acceptance levels of America are rich in such freedom. How tragic it would be if fundamentalist thinking and regression to earlier times increased prejudice, intolerance, and the loss of our spiritual freedom.

The effects of regression to earlier times can be observed in England and the soccer riots of 1985. During a soccer game in Belgium, English hooligans (angry, violent English youth from street gangs) caused violent riots resulting in hundreds of spectator deaths. These riots continued for some years. These hooligans were an expression of an England that had regressed to more traditional and primitive lifestyles. The same dangers need to be guarded against happening in our country.

There is edginess in America caused by terrorism, economic slumps, uncertainty of corporations, falling consumer confidence and so on. While President Bush has, as of this writing, negotiated a United Nations resolution dealing with Iraq, Washington's policy seems to present tones of war as an inevitability and forgone conclusion.

The Muslim world also wants change in Iraq. However, the United States is the last country from which it wants it. The Arab world may embrace democracy (Elliot, 2002) but it is not accepting America's version, if it accepts democracy at all. Deputy Secretary of Defense Paul Wolfowitz is seeking a transformation in the Middle East (Elliot, 2002). However, there is pessimism as to whether the United States is in a position to remodel the world on its own.

Unilateralism cannot create the kind of spiritual contextualization needed to uproot terrorism and empower transforming seeds of cultural motifs. Elliot (2002) argues that the transformation of Europe was inspired by what President Reagan stood for, not what he said. The transforming power of example is the West's freedom and prosperity. The transformation of tyranny is inspired by heartfelt decisions, not overpowering ideologies (Elliot, 2002). Arab families, like European and American families, want their children to lead a better life.

Instead of forcing people of diverse nations to choose between freedom and patriotism, internal pressures for nurturing and encouraging cultural motifs resolve this Gordian knot of bipolar politics. Creating a global contextualization that enhances the proliferation of empowering, cultural motifs is essential to transformation. Cultural motifs contain the core spiritual seeds that bring to fruition the best in each culture. A globalization that creates a context of healthy, stimulating, dialectical exchange creates a global metamotif (e.g., a motif of motif transformation). Such a global metamotif transcends international market-states, corporations, and undue nationalistic interests. Globalizations of such quality go further to erode the roots of terrorism than the most powerful military, corporate enterprise, or nationalistic self-protectionism. Preventative and anticipatory efforts to create a revisioning for a new millennium require transformational alterations at core levels of our national and cultural identities. Rooting out terrorism means rooting in strength and prosperity in a global garden where all cultural motifs can mature to fruition. Healthy and respectful dialectical exchange in a global context that nurtures temporal and spatial openness for all cultural motifs empowers transformation. Cultural motifs have the inherent resilience for transformation of global communities into a wondrous mosaic of metamotifs. The fertile ground of a healthy global context and the nurturing rain of refreshing dialectical exchanges are the sustenance of transformational, cultural motifs.

EPILOGUE: GETTING OUT OF THE IN-BOX

This work addresses the critical need for global transformation through dialectical exchanges of cultural motifs. The challenge of these exchanges involves a paradoxical dilemma. Cultural motifs involve experiential qualities of subjective identification. That is, Americans obviously identify themselves with all the sights, sounds, feelings, sensations and so on of what it means to be an American. While we may cognitively grasp that people of other cultures will act and speak according to their own motif, being experientially grounded in the subjective reality of American identity can confine us to a kind of tunnel vision or box. How do people grounded in one reality of their unique culture's motif simultaneously step outside their own subjective, self-affirming box and into another? It is not unlike the days of Galileo and Copernicus proclaiming that Earth was not the center of the universe and there were more planets in the solar system than believed by the Catholic Church. This was considered blasphemous and heretical, violating religious beliefs.

The paradox thus emerges: How can people from one cultural motif exchange and genuinely interact when blinded to other motifs by the one in which they already occupy? There needs to be a state of suspension (releasing one's perceptual grip on an experiential level) so that their subjective reality is not the center of the universe of world affairs. While we may give lip service to diversity, understanding the unique reality of other cultures continues to remain a foreign experience. Witness the rise in prejudice against the Jews in Europe, the continued antagonism in the

Mideast, and the shock and terror of America to 9/11! The shock and amazement of why other cultures are so negative toward America reflect the foreign nature of one culture to another.

How can we experience another reality while still holding on to the one we have? Without some release of a culture's grip that its motif is the only reality, dialectical exchange is quite difficult. This release or suspension is what the Catholic Church went through in working through the challenges to its universe as created by the God of that day.

The working through of new orderings and the redesign of present reality to a higher-ordering transformation are known as phase transitions. Kaku (1994) writes in his book *Hyperspace* that the universe (read people, countries, and cultures as well as atoms and quantum particles) operates in a false vacuum (i.e., a symmetry that does not accurately reflect deep reality). He referred to the Iranian (Muslim) physicist Vafa, who first proposed a strong theory of the universe indicating there were actually 10, not 4, dimensions (e.g., three spatial and one temporal) of deep reality.

An example of a false vacuum where a proposed symmetry of reality inaccurately fits is trying to stretch a bedsheet with elastic corners on a bed that is too large for it. Every time the attempt is made to force the smaller bedsheet onto the larger bed, one of the sheet's elastic corners snaps off. This snapping is when the proposed symmetry breaks, goes into a phase transition, and a newer, higher ordering is required. Such breaks in symmetry occur in the life stages (Erikson, 1950) of human beings from childhood to our experience of world affairs. As the world ordering evolves and matures, newer, higher-ordering configurations (e.g., formativeness) are required. It is when something snaps out of shape (or motif) that there are signs that the times are a'changing. The new formativeness requires this snap or release to be where present symmetry (e.g., ways of making sense of our world) needs to be reconfigured (e.g., marriage, divorce, empty-nest syndrome, or globalization).

The word "formation" means education in French. It is the resultant effect of learning and experience in forming, re-forming, and transforming the student. It brings out the genuine potential formativeness (e.g., unique motif) that is what he or she and culture are inherently informed to be.

Achieving a globalization that informs and transforms each culture's motif into an interactive, global mosaic or tapestry requires learning, experience, and, above all, safe space-time frames. The latter is needed to provide a secure forum for release in phase transitions that allow for dialectical exchange and interactivity. Models of dialectic exchange need to be developed (e.g., within and beyond America's diversity) that prove to be reliable and valid forums for genuine learning to occur.

The focus needs to be directed toward core qualities of what makes each cultural motif so unique. This transcends ritual, fashion, and language idioms (yet certainly includes these and more) and targets unique, schematic design structures that constitute motifs.

As learning and education are required to develop new ways of experiencing other cultures (e.g., formativeness), the sensory systems are critical. Experiencing the different ways cultural motifs structure and design their linguistic patterns, imagery, emotional templates, and sensory representations facilitates dialectical exchange. Receiving a letter from The French Institute on Higher Education, I was struck to notice that its stationery was longer and thinner than American business stationery. The envelopes are also shorter and narrower than American envelopes. In addition, while American letters end with "sincerely yours," French formal letters end in lengthy complimentary closings that emphasize distinguishing and lofty considerations. These are just a few of the unique sensory (physical and linguistic) experiences that hint at core cultural uniqueness.

Only by comparing, contrasting, and experiencing the unique differences (e.g., a willingness to suspend judgment and one's grip on one's inaccurate symmetry for deep reality) can genuine dialectical exchange occur. Literally, by holding French and American letterhead side by side were the unique, subtle differences highlighted and appreciated. Instead of trying to homogenize and cookie-cut all motifs as one, cultural respect and dialectical exchange are enhanced by grasping unique differences that give quality to each culture. We may be fundamentally the same, but it is our unique differences that enrich the mosaic of cultural motifs. It is the unique characteristics of each culture's motif that facilitate the interactive dialogue that creates meaningful respect and relatedness. The universe is an unfolding, divine mystery of artistic tapestries, unfolded in its becoming while perfect in its conception. Cultural motifs reflect and refract such artistry. Grasping the unique mystery and wonder of each culture's artistic motifs brings them out of the museums and into the diplomacy of the human street.

The Romanian language has a word *omenia*, which means the manner of being humane. In Romanian, hospitality and being humane involve laying out a delicate spread of sausages, cheeses, and breads on a lace cloth. Pronouncing the word "omenia" involves that sounds "ohm" (as in meditation) and "enia" (meaning the manner of doing something like setting a table of food). The "ohm" sound is the same sound for the French word "homme" (meaning "man"). Therefore, what one uniquely experiences in saying this word is both the literal (e.g., the sensory sound of "ohm") and figural (symbolic reference) merger of sensory and cognitive experience. It is just such a congruent merger of unique sensory experience (e.g., the sound of "humane") and the reference to humane manner (e.g., working definition) that is the artistry of its unique, cultural motif. Indeed, the "omenia" of unique, artistic cultural motifs is the humane manner in which we learn to respect and treat one another. Design structures of sensory experience embodied into symbolic meaning breathe life energy into transformative, cultural motifs. It is this transformative core energy of cultural motifs that can synergize a release of symmetry to a higher ordering of global contextualization. Fusion (e.g., hydrogen bonding as in the Sun's power) is a coming together as energy is released. The power of synergy is the release of energy in the dialectical exchange of unique elements of interfacing core motifs. It is by exchanging our unique, interfacing motifs that meaningful transformations in a terror-ridden world can breathe life into the divine mystery of our global artistry. Is this not the purpose for which we are here?

BIBLIOGRAPHY

Ansbacher, H. L., & Ansbacher, R. R. (1956). *The individual psychology of Alfred Adler.* New York: Harper & Row.

Appadurai, A. (2002, September/October). Broken promises. *Foreign Policy,* (132), 42–44.

Ausubel, J. H. (1993, November/December). 2020 vision. *The Sciences,* 16–18.

Bloom, H. (1995). *The Lucifer principle.* New York: Atlantic Monthly Press.

Bobbit, P. (2002, September 9). Get ready for the next long war. *Time, 160*(11), 84–85.

Brown, D. P., & Fromm, E. (1986). *Hypnotherapy and hypoanalysis.* Hillsdale, NJ: Lawrence Erlbaum Assoc., Inc.

Brown, W. R. (1980). *The last crusade.* Chicago: Nelson-Hall.

Buber, M. (1958). *I and thou.* New York: Charles Scribner's Sons.

Chomsky, N. (1967). Recent contributions to the theory of innate ideas. *Synthese,* (17), 23–29.

Chomsky, N. (2001). *9–11.* New York: Seven Stories Press.

Cloud, J. (2001, October 8). Atta's odyssey. *Time, 158*(16), 64–67.

Csikszentmihalyi, M. (1990). *Flow.* New York: Harper & Row.

Dabrowski, K. (1967). *Personality shaping through positive disintegration.* Boston: Little, Brown.

Dabrowski, K. (1970). Positive and accelerated development. In K. Dabrowski, A. Kawczak, & M. M. Piechowski (Eds.), *Mental growth through positive disintegration.* London: Gryf.

Dabrowski, K., & Piechowski, M. M. (1977). *Theory of levels of emotional development: Multilevelness and positive disintegration* (Vol. 1). Oceanside, NY: Dabor Science Publications.

DeSousa. (2002) *What's so great about America.* Washington DC: Regnery Pub.

Douglas, J. (1995). *Mind hunter.* New York: Pocket Books.

Dublin, F. (1973, May). *The problem, who speaks next? Considered cross-culturally.* Paper presented at the meeting of TESOL (Translations in English, Spanish and Other Languages). San Juan, Puerto Rico.

Ebersole, P., & Quiring, G. (1991). Meaning in life depth: The MILD. *Journal of Humanistic Psychology, 31*(3), 113–124.

Edelman, G. M. (1992). *Bright air, brilliant fire: On the matter of the mind.* New York: Basic Books.

Egger, S. A. (1984). A working definition of serial murder and the reduction of linkage blindness. *Journal of Police Science and Administration, 12*(3), 348–357.

Eliot, L. (1999). *What's going on in there?* New York: Bantam.

Elliot, M. (2001, November 12). Hate club. *Time, 158*(21), 58–74.

Elliot, M. (2002, November 4). Do they want something better? *Time, 160*(19), 116.

Erikson, E. H. (1950). *Childhood and society.* New York: Norton.

Etcoff, N. (1999). *Survival of the prettiest.* New York: Basic Books.

Feeney, D. J., Jr. (1996). The purposeful self. *Journal of Humanistic Psychology, 36*(4), 94–115.

Feeney, D. J., Jr. (1999), *Entrancing relationships.* Westport, CT: Praeger Press.

Feeney, D. J., Jr. (2001). *Motifs: The transformative creation of self.* Westport, CT: Praeger.

Feeney, K. L. (2001). *Reiki healing session personal consultation.* In D. J. Feeney Jr., *Motifs: The transformative creation of self.* Westport, CT: Praeger.

Frankl, V. (1963). *Man's search for meaning.* New York: Washington Square.

Garfinkle, A. (2002, Fall). The impossible imperative? Conjuring Arab democracy. *The National Interest,* (69), 156–166.

Gilman, T. (2002). An era of peaceful relations. *Renaissance Magazine, 7*(27), 48.

Gilman, T. (2002). The prosperity and tolerance of Muslim Spain. *Renaissance Magazine, 7*(27), 45–48.

Gilman, T. (2002). An era of peaceful relations. *Renaissance Magazine, 7*(27), 48.

Hall, E. T. (1974). *Handbook for proxemic research.* Washington DC: Society for the Ontology of Visual Communication.

Hassner, P. (2002, Fall). Definitions, doctrines, and divergences. *The National Interest,* (69), 30–34.

James, T., & Woodsmall, W. (1988). *Timeline therapy.* Cupertino, CA: Meta Publications.

Jansen, J. V. (1985). Perspective on non-verbal intercultural communication. In L. A. Sumovar & R. E. Porter (Eds.), *Intercultural communication: A reader,* Belmont, CA: Wadsworth.

Jung, C. G. (1971). *Psychological types.* Princeton: Princeton University Press.

Kaku, M. (1994). *Hyperspace.* New York: Doubleday.

Kant, I. (1998). *Groundwork of the metaphysics of morals* (H.J. Paton, Trans.). New Haven, CT: Yale University Text.

Kelley, L. (2002). *Motivation.* Morgan Hill, CA: Grow Pub.

Krauthammer, C. (2001, December 24). Only in their dreams. *Time, 158*(27), 60–61.

Kupchan, C. (2002, Fall). Misreading Sept. 11th. *The National Interest,* (69), 26–30.

Lee, K.Y. (1996, Winter). America is no longer Asia's model. *New Perspectives Quarterly.*

Leonard, M. (2002). Diplomacy by other means. *Foreign Policy,* (132), 48–56.

Ludwig, A.M. (1966). Altered states of consciousness. *Archives of General Psychiatry, 15,* 225–234.

MacCulloch, M., Snowden, P., Wood, P., & Mills, E. (1983). Sadistic fantasy, sadistic behavior and offending. *British Journal Psychiatry, 143,* 20–29.

Maslow, A. (1968). *Towards a psychology of being.* New York: Harper.

Mehrabian, A. (1972). *Non-verbal communication.* Chicago: Aldene-Atherton.

Mehrabian, A., & Ferris, S.R. (1976). Influence of attitudes from non-verbal communication in two channels. *Journal of Consulting Psychology, 31,* 248–252.

Mocuta, M. (2001). L'oeil écoute. *Claudel Studies, 28.* Irving, TX: University of Dallas.

Mondschein, K., & Steinsaltz, D. (2002). The greatest minds of the age. *Renaissance Magazine, 7, 3*(27), 42.

Moore, T. (1992). *Care of the soul.* New York: Harper Collins.

Naim, M. (2002). Post-terror surprises. *Foreign Policy,* (132).

News Poll. (2002, September 2). *The New York Times.*

News Poll. (2002, November 17). *American Broadcasting Corporation.*

Nye, J.S. (1990, Fall). Soft Power. *Foreign Policy.*

Pearce, J.C. (1986). *Magical child matures.* New York: Bantam Books.

Pelayo, C. (2002). The woman behind the prophet. *Renaissance Magazine, 7, 3*(27), 32.

Piaget, J., & Inhelder, B. (1964). *The early growth of logic in the child.* Atlantic Highlands, NJ: Humanities Press.

Pipes, D. (2002). *Militant Islam reaches America.* New York: W.W. Norton & Co.

Prentky, R., Burgess, A., & Carter, D. (1986). Victim responses by rapist type: An empirical and clinical analysis. *Journal of Interpersonal Violence, 1,* 73–98.

Rammelkamp, C. (2002). The thousand years of Islam. *Renaissance Magazine, 7, 3*(27), 29–36.

Rammelkamp, C. (2002). Striving for jihad. *Renaissance Magazine, 7, 3*(27), 31.

Rammelkamp, C. (2002). The schism between Sunni vs. Shi'e Islam. *Renaissance Magazine, 7, 3*(27), 36.

Restak, R. (1995). *Brainscapes.* New York: Bantam Books.

Riyadh, S. M. (2001, November 19). The near misses. *Time,* 57.

Rogoff, B. (2003). *Cultural nature of human development.* Oxford: Oxford Academic Trade.

Rubin, B. (2002). The real roots of Arab anti-Americanism. *Foreign Affairs, 81*(6), 73–85.

Russett, B. (1992). *The Carnegie committee for science technology and government task force.* New Haven, CT: Yale University.

Russett, B. (1993, November). Peace among democracies. *Scientific American,* (120).

Santos, M. (2002). The Arabian nights: A tale of the people. *Renaissance Magazine, 7, 3*(27), 54–57.

Schlesinger, L. B., & Revitch, E. (1980). The criminal fantasy technique: A comparison of sex offenders and substance abusers. *Journal of Clinical Psychology, 37,* 210–218.

Searle, J. R. (1997). *The mystery of consciousness.* New York: New York Review of Books.

Seiden, E. (2002). The Muslim impact on medieval Europe. *Renaissance Magazine, 7, 3*(27), 38–42.

Smith, N. F., & LeZotte, P. (2002). *Paralle'les: Communication et culture* (2nd ed.). Upper Saddle River, NJ: Prentice-Hall, Inc.

Stiglitz, J. (2002). *Globalization and its discontents.* New York: Harbinger Press.

Sue, D. W., & Sue, D. (1990). *Counseling the culturally different: Theory and practice* (2nd ed.). New York: John Wiley & Sons, Inc.

Tart, C. T. (1969). *Altered states of consciousness.* New York: John Wiley and Sons, Inc.

Tucker, K. (2001, November 2). The importance of being Dave. *Entertainment,* (623), 26.

Tucker, R. W. (2002). One year on power, purpose, and strategy in American foreign policy. *The National Interest,* (69), 5–7.

VanBiema, D. (2002, September 30). The legacy of Abraham. *Time, 160*(14), 64–85.

Wholey, D. (1988). *Becoming your own parent.* New York: Doubleday.

Williams, B. (2003, March 15). *CNBC Nightly News.* National Broadcasting Corporation.

Woodward, K. L. (2000). *The book of miracles.* New York: Simon & Schuster.

Zakaria, F. (1994, March/April). A conversation with Lee Kuan Yew. *Foreign Affairs.*

Zakaria, F. (2001, October 15). Why do they hate us? *Newsweek, 138*(16), 22–40.

INDEX

About the Author

DON J. FEENEY JR. is a clinical psychologist and certified drug and alcohol counselor, as well as a certified neurolinguistic programmer. He is Founder and Director of Consulting Psychological Services in Chicago and the author of two previous Praeger books, *Entrancing the Relationships* and *Motifs: The Transformation Creation of Self.*